Daughters of Eve

A resounding call to recapture God's glorious vision for women

Lyn Packer

Daughters of Eve
Lyn Packer

Copyright © 2019 Lyn Packer

ISBN 978-0-473-52029-8 - Softcover
ISBN 978-0-473-52031-1 - Kindle

All rights reserved.
This book was published by Lyn Packer, New Zealand,
under Rob and Lyn Packer Ministries.
No part of this book may be reproduced in any form, by any means, without the express permission of the author. This includes reprints, photocopying, recording, or any future means of reproducing text.

If you would like to use any part of this book in articles, teachings, or any other means of recording or media, you must seek permission first by contacting me at office@robandlyn.org

Website – www.robandlyn.org

All Scriptures unless otherwise noted are taken from the King James Version or the NIV. Scripture quotations are taken from the Holy Bible, New International Version®, NIV®. Copyright © 1973, 1978, 1984, 2011 by Biblica, Inc.™ Used by permission of Zondervan.
All rights reserved worldwide. www.zondervan.com The "NIV" and "New International Version" are trademarks registered in the United States Patent and Trademark Office by Biblica, Inc.™
Cover Design by Lyn Packer

Contents

Endorsements	5
Introduction	11
1. Remembering Eve	13
2. God's Original Plan	15
3. Consequences Of The Fall	31
4. Before Jesus	44
5. Jesus – Back To The Original Plan	54
6. The Early Church	62
7. Paul's Tricky verses	67
8. From Jesus And Paul To Today	82
9. Where We Are Today	94
10. Into The Future	107
How To Use This Book As A Study Guide	116
Author's Bio	122

Endorsements

In these days God is raising up and equipping an army to bring a huge number of people into the kingdom and prepare them for full maturity in Jesus Christ. Lyn Packer's book *Daughters of Eve* specifically addresses the spiritual foundations and processes for the full development of women in the kingdom of God. She combines a heartfelt love for God with thoughtful analysis of both Scripture and human experience to help women be free to achieve their God given destinies. I believe this book will be of great benefit to many women.
Joan Hunter
Author/evangelist
TV Host Miracles Happen!
www.joanhunter.org

• • • ● • • •

Lyn Packer has written an extraordinarily important book that will strengthen marriages, families, and churches. In *Daughters of Eve* she reveals how much we have lost on account of sin and how much we can now enjoy on account of Jesus. Written for men as much as women, this is a book to inspire and guide us back to God's glorious plan. A must read.
Paul Ellis
Author and director of Escape to Reality
www.escapetoreality.org

• • • ● • • •

Lyn Packer is surely packing a truth bomb that explodes in *Daughters of Eve*! Man or woman, I believe you will be both challenged and inspired as you process some of the profound revelation that is captured in this volume. If your heart is open and attentive to what the Holy Spirit is saying, the words of this book may give you a gentle indoctrination detox, and you just might find yourself refreshed! I pray that all – especially the men – who read these words will deeply consider their power and seek to be the change. "Daughters of Eve" is one of many glorious sparks responsible for igniting a fresh reformation in the church and society today! -
Rob Radosti - Founder, Church14
www.church14.com

For over 40 years Lyn, along with her husband Rob, have consistently ministered the gospel in one capacity or another, and the depth of prophetic revelation and ministry they carry just continues to increase. What a gift they are!

In this season, God is using people with the right heart and skills for the purpose of revealing his original masterpiece in all its glory. This book *Daughters of Eve* is part of that work. I love this book, but at the same time it created uncomfortable emotions in me as I read it. I found I needed to deal with some areas and forgive, mostly those who had no idea of what they were doing. I also recognize it is the enemy who is the cause of all this – he is the father of lies, and seeks to steal, kill and destroy. And he's been busy.

I deeply admire Lyn for writing this book. She is one who has faced difficulties and barriers in her calling as a prophet, yet she has remained true to her calling when many have given up. As a woman of integrity, she demonstrates grace and understanding, and there is no hook or agenda here. Rather, this is an honest investigation to discover truth. I heartily recommend this book to all who wish to understand the roles of both men and women, (according to God's original intent) and how both history and traditions can bring distortion.

Dayle Wright
Senior Leader, Invercargill Christian Centre,
New Zealand Bethel Sozo Facilitator
www.christiancentre.org.nz
www.bethelsozonewzealand.com

* * * ● ● * *

Lyn asked me to write an endorsement for her new book *Daughters of Eve* but unfortunately because of busyness I was unable to do so, but I offer this to you as an endorsement. I have known Lyn Packer for many years and love her heart for the Lord and for His people. She is wonderfully prophetic, creative and committed to presenting and imparting truth. I recommend her as a faithful minister and steward of the Word.

Patricia King
Leader of Patricia King Ministries, Author,
Television Host and Christian Minister
www.patriciakingministries.com

I am many things – a male pastor, a business owner and commercial fisherman. I've worked in the wildest, remotest, marine area of southern New Zealand for 25 yrs. In my walk with God some of my greatest encouragers have been women. Some of the most 'in touch with God', Spirit filled, mentors I have met are women, e.g. Joyce Meyer, Patricia King, Heidi Baker, Lyn Packer, and more. They have each inspired me deeply.

There is a doctrine held by some which says that God says women should not preach or lead men in any way, but wherever I look today I see women prophets, apostles, pastors, teachers, and evangelists who have been called into these offices by God, ministering with so much good fruit in evidence. God is blessing these ministries, so it appears to me that if God is blessing their ministries then maybe we've got something wrong in that church doctrine. I also minister in some cultures that hold women in very low esteem both culturally, and in the church. I constantly see women in those situations that have God-given gifts and callings, sitting limply on the floor with no opportunity to do anything, while men are given the chance to minister or given positions of authority simply because they are men.

This very brave book by Lyn Packer will shake that "Woman are inferior and have no place in leadership" doctrine to the core, giving us much needed insight and understanding into what God's plan for women is, and has always been. Lyn may take many hits for this book by keyboard warriors and people confronted by her revelations and the truth she brings to the light, but Lyn, as a "fully man's man", I applaud you! As a man and a Pastor I will stand by you, and defend you with all I have.

This is a book with a word for today and the times we are journeying into. It will shake everything that has been believed about women and Christian ministry, and some will rage, and some will repent. May you be one of the latter and, along with me, help raise these "wonder women" to their rightful, God blessed and anointed place, and smile with me as they arise and shine.

John Steffens MNZM
(Member of the New Zealand Order of Merit)
Senior Leader
Fiordland New Life Church

Mankind, much like its Maker, has an amazing ability to create a way into places that we wouldn't normally be able to go. For example, much of the ocean freezes over and becomes impassable to boats and ships. But instead of leaving these places as uncharted waters we created *Icebreakers*. These vessels are designed with a special purpose – to navigate through ice-covered waters, and provide safe waterways for other boats and ships. Not only can they cut through impassable waters, but they create a way for others to follow in behind them and make the impossible possible. They break through the barriers that have prevented so many others from achieving their goals and following the road they feel to travel.

Lyn Packer is one of God's *special-purpose icebreakers*. She has an amazing ability to travel through places and break through terrain that would crush most people. She has created numerous pathways for the body of Christ to travel what were previously uncharted waters. In both the prophetic and the creative arts Lyn has cut tracks that many have journeyed on since and will continue to travel on for generations to come. This book *Daughters of Eve* is yet another snapshot of a track that Lyn has been cutting into the icy waters of the restoration of woman in the church and in society.

We love Lyn and have watched her live this message for many years. She has been carrying the warmth of the Father's love into these icy waters for decades, all whilst continuing in humility, kindness, and honour with incredible grace – even in the midst of opposition and accusation. We are grateful for this book and for the person that it comes from – Enjoy!

Josh & Amberley Klinkenberg
Inflame Ministries
Sounds of the Nations Directors for New Zealand
www.inflameministries.com

• • • ● • •

Women have been a part of God's plan since the beginning (see Genesis 1:26-28). And that has not changed. Look at how the Victorious Risen Lord launched a woman out into an apostolic preaching ministry when He gave Mary a message with the instructions to go and share it with the brothers (see John 20:11-18). Or how the Apostle Paul put a woman into a leadership position in the church while encouraging others to honor and support her in that role (see Romans 16:1-2). If any of that rankles you or is hard for you to get your head around, then you for sure need to read Lyn Packer's book *Daughters of Eve*.

It will help you come to see women the way God sees them: as His amazing and wonderful creations who are dearly loved, and absolutely capable of operating in any and all of His callings, gifts and assignment. Thank you, Lyn, for writing a book that puts women in their place – right in the midst of everything God is doing!

Robert Hotchkin
Robert Hotchkin Ministries
Men on the Frontlines
www.roberthotchkin.com

* * * ● * * *

Daughters of Eve is a game-changing book for churches and church leaders brave enough to admit that just repeating what we have always heard, known and copied, has not done much to release generations of women to the call of God on their lives. We have watched as women have been honoured on the mission field but minimised as they have come home to tell of what God is doing in and through their call and lives.

If male leaders are honest they know little of early church history, theology and inherited culture bias towards the 'Daughters of Eve', which is continued to be reflected and repeated in church leadership teams throughout the world.

I cannot recommend this book highly enough as it is a modern day theses nailed to church doors everywhere. Thank you Lyn for your bravery, grace, and journey found in these pages.

Ian Wright
Senior Leader
Invercargill Christian Centre and Wright Ministries
www.christiancentre.org.nz

* * * ● * * *

I believe that we are living in a season where women, as never before, have the opportunity to take places at leadership and influence in society. However, for woman to thrive in the season, the subtle background beliefs and messages that frame cultural norms must be confronted and reconsidered. Lyn Packer invites you to do so in her new book *Daughters of Eve*. This book is well researched, and well laid out, but what makes it a great read is much more than that. My measurement of a truly good book is the degree to which calls me into the narrative and elicits strong emotion in me. This book did both, provoking a range of feelings and me that started with shock, and anger, and evolved into compassion and hope as Lyn invited me to journey through the history of women and their place in our world.

In *Daughters of Eve*, Lyn invites you to investigate and reconsider the historical facts regarding women, their role in the Bible and their place in God's ultimate plan for His church. This book will change the way you think, and I highly recommend it for women throughout the body of Christ, and the men who walk with them.

Wendy Peter
Director - Women on the Frontlines Global.
www.wendypeter.com
www.wimnglobal.com

Introduction

The subject this book addresses is a critical aspect of theology that we need to grapple with for the era we live in. More than ever before we need the church to be functioning at full capacity, with every member doing their part and being free to fulfil the call of God that is on their lives.

Let me take a moment to share with you why I've written this book. I approach this subject not just as a Bible study, but also for very personal reasons. The first of these is that I am a woman. I'm a woman who wanted to know the truth about my identity as a woman, how God saw me, and what His plans for my life were. I wanted to be in right relationship – with God and with the church. It was also very personal for other reasons, as you'll read later in this book in the chapter which tells my story.

But this book is not just important to me; the content of this book is important to us all. The church worldwide cannot avoid looking at the subject of a woman's role in church and society and the implications it has had, and continues to have.

I'm not a recognised theologian, just a woman trying to understand her place in God's order of things. I don't have a fancy degree in writing so this book doesn't pretend to be an all-encompassing, comprehensive deep-dive into everything Scripture says on the subject of women – that would be a very big book and would need to be written by someone other than me. But, I have researched deeply and faithfully, and this book does cover the major questions that arise in our minds as we read the verses in the Bible about women and their role, and it seeks to show what Scripture really says about those things. In my study of this subject and preparation for writing this book I have always tried my best to remain as impartial as

I could, and have done my best to seek out the truth. My desire has been genuinely to discover what God had originally planned for women and what He expects of me as a woman.

As you read this book I pray that your desire would be to discover God's glorious plans for women and to allow your mind to be stretched, your beliefs challenged and your freedom expanded. One of the ways you can do this is by engaging with, and thinking through, the questions at the end of each chapter as I have formatted the book to also be used as a study guide by both individuals and groups. You can find how to use the book for group study in the chapter at the end of the book.

It is now many years since I first started researching and studying this topic and I still find stuff that astounds me. Little did I know that what I was to discover as I studied would blow apart much of what I'd been taught and believed over the years. All those years ago I genuinely believed that I was following God's will in viewing women through the viewpoint presented as the universally accepted, traditional church teaching. But as I studied I saw that God's plan was infinitely far greater than what I'd been taught. Today God is revealing the truth that was always there in Scripture and is restoring women to their original place in His grand plan for mankind. As a result women everywhere are rediscovering God's original plan for them, coming into a place of true freedom and are following God's call on their lives and making this world a better place.

Through this book I pray that the glory of being a woman would be restored for those who read it, and that people would recognize the beauty and power in which we were created as an image bearer, a strong help, a light, and as a unique expression of the living God. I invite you to journey with me into understanding and freedom, to discover for yourself the reality that in Christ there is neither Jew nor Greek, slave nor free, male nor female, but that we are actually all equal and one in Christ.

1
Remembering Eve – The Mother Of Mankind

I've long been fascinated by this first woman and what she was really like. Oh I know what I've been told about her over the years – she was deceived, she was a temptress, she caused the fall of the human race – but who was she actually? What was she like? I can glean very little from Scripture so most of what I think about her can only be suppositions made on my part. Scripture tells us very little about what she and Adam were like – their personalities or their physical descriptions. Science and geographical clues tell us that they were probably reasonably dark skinned and that all women still carry a DNA marker that can be traced back to her, but apart from that I am still left largely with my suppositions and imagination to somehow build a picture of what she was like. I do know, however, that my thoughts about her will always fall far short of the glory she carried, the dignity she had as one made in God's image, the authority she carried and walked in, the beauty of the innocence she had, and the relationship she had with both God and Adam.

My thoughts will also fall far short of understanding the grief she must have suffered when she lost all that she once walked in, the devastation and consequences that happened when she and Adam sinned and took part in the act that caused them both to fall from the place of innocence and trust that they enjoyed. Those consequences were huge, and both she and Adam lost so much, as did we who followed after them. I can only imagine the feelings and grief over the loss of innocence, of trust, of their glory, the loss of their ability to access the garden in Eden and the brokenness that entered their relationship with God. And again my imagination of that probably falls far short of the reality of it, even though I personally have faced devastation and loss in my life.

My hope is that in some small way this book shows a small part of the debt we have all owed her, because no matter what happened, or who was to blame, there would be no human race without her. No matter what race or culture we are from, we all owe our existence to this one woman, Eve. For that fact alone – that we live and breathe – we should be eternally grateful to her for her part in that.

I think of her sometimes as I give thanks for the life that I get to live, the air I get to breathe, the blood that flows through my veins, the ability to carry another human being in my womb and co-create them with my spouse and with God. I am thankful that because of her I get the chance to be alive and one day I look forward to being able to say that to her face-to-face.

Go deeper

- How have you viewed Eve up until this point in time?
- Have you tended to hold her primarily responsible for mankind's condition?
- Have you forgiven her and Adam for the effect their sin had on society over the years, on your life, and on the church?

2
God's Original Plan

Let's start with the Trinity

What are the Trinity like – The Father, Jesus and Holy Spirit? Do we really know, or do we simply believe what we've been told down through the centuries? When I first started to dig into a deeper understanding of what the Trinity were like it was like twin bombs going off – one was a bomb that destroyed a lot of the beliefs I had held until that time, and the other was a bomb of excitement. Suddenly the Trinity made more sense, and what I found confirmed something I instinctively knew inside my heart of hearts – as a woman I had been made in the image of the Trinity!

In most of this book I'll be using the term God to refer to the Trinity, as it is the most common term used by the church to describe them. The Trinity – God, Jesus and Holy Spirit – are understood to be Spirit, yet we try to fit them into our human boxes of understanding about gender, trying to make them like us, male and/or female. The Trinity do have both masculine and feminine aspects to their characteristics and expressions; Scripture very clearly supports that, when we look deeper than just our modern English texts; we could not be made in their image if this is not so.

Most of the modern church believe in an all-male Trinity – God the Father, Jesus His son, and the other man, the Holy Spirit. Yet that is not what the ancient Hebrews, or the early church, believed. They believed that the Trinity had what we would call both masculine and feminine characteristics to their nature, as you will see as you read on. In reality the Trinity transcend our classifications of gender; they are not human, but in order to try and understand them we make comparisons to the genders we have here on earth – male and female. These comparisons give us some ideas of God, but do not, and cannot, ever give us the complete picture; some things will always remain not fully understandable by us, and we have to be okay with that.

But back to my attempt to try and bring some understanding. In Scripture we see many attempts to portray God's character, and many of those are shown in the names of God found in Scripture. We see Jesus refer to God as Father, but another name given to God in Scripture is El Shaddai. The words El Shaddai relate to the breast and the womb[1] and give the idea that God is the source of our life, but also the powerful nurturer. In our modern translations this name El Shaddai has been translated Almighty God, but the actual meaning of that name is about being a powerful nurturer[2].

Two different, but complementary, pictures of God emerge from these two descriptions – of God having what we know as both masculine and feminine characteristics.

But why did Jesus refer to God as 'God our Father'? Was He saying that God was a male? The Jews up until that time knew God by other names or terms, such as 'the God of Abraham, Isaac and Jacob'. When that term was first used it was used by those who knew these men, but over the centuries it came to mean the God of our ancestors, an impersonal distant God. Jesus was deliberate in the terms He used, and the term Father conveyed not gender, but source, intimacy and close relationship. He was saying that God is where we come from, we are God's children. God is our source and His relationship with us is like a father's relationship. Jesus also spoke of God using feminine terminology when He described God as being like a woman who searched for her lost coin, and in the parable where the woman puts yeast in a loaf of bread. In Isa 42:13–14 we see God described both in male and female terms, where God is described as a mighty man marching into battle, and as a woman giving birth.

In Scripture we see that Jesus is referred to as the Son of God and the Son of mankind, and we know that He took on a male physical form on earth.

Holy Spirit is generally believed by most Christians to be yet another masculine being. However, when we look at Hebrew culture and literature, their understanding has always been that the Spirit of God was feminine in characteristics and they referred to the Spirit in feminine terms.[3] Throughout the Old Testament the words used to describe Holy Spirit are in most cases feminine; partly that's because Hebrew is a gendered language and partly it's because they believed the Spirit of God had feminine characteristics. The Hebrew language has nouns that are masculine and feminine, but that doesn't necessarily mean that the objects themselves are male or female.

The New Testament was written in Greek because that was the language used by scribes and scholars of their time, and the Greek word for Spirit is neuter, or genderless, in characteristic and nature, and means 'that one, or thing'. However, when it came to translating the original documents into the Bible we know and read today, for some reason the translators ignored both the Hebrew and Greek meanings of the word and assigned a male identity to Holy Spirit. Here's a couple of verses that show that male gender assignment, as found in our English translations.

"I will ask the Father, and He will give you another Helper, that He [that one] may be with you forever" John 14:16

"[13] But when He [that one], the Spirit of truth, comes, He [that one] will guide you into all the truth; for He [that one] will not speak on His [that one's] own initiative, but whatever He [that one] hears, He [that one] will speak; and He [that one] will disclose to you what is to come. [14]"He [that one] will glorify Me, for He [that one] will take of Mine and will disclose it to you." John 16:13-14

Scripture tells us in Genesis 1 that the Holy Spirit was there at creation, brooding over the chaos, and bringing life into being. We also see Lady Wisdom recorded in Scripture as being there at creation. Wisdom speaks of herself as being "beside" Yahweh (Prov 8:30) when He created the world. In Isaiah 11:2-3 the seven-fold Spirit of God is referred to as the Spirit of Wisdom. Many ancient theologians and historians, including Origen, Jerome and Irenaeus, propose that Wisdom and Holy Spirit are the same divine feminine being. They have identical roles and functions, both are feminine, and both are present in the beginning.[4]

When Christianity made the transition from mostly Hebrew-speaking

Israelites to also including Greek-speaking gentiles, any feminine references to the nature of Holy Spirit were gradually lost in translation into Greek language and understanding. Once the 4th century creeds were written the Holy Spirit became part of an all-masculine Trinity, and the spiritual implications of the feminine Spirit had also disappeared.

Throughout history we see man's efforts to try and explain the nature and character of the Trinity, but our best efforts tend to confine them, rather than define them. The Trinity, or God, as we collectively know them, are expressed as being masculine, and as being feminine or nurturing as well. This understanding of God's essence, that of being the fullness of both male and female characteristics and expression, is where we get our original understanding that family originated with God.

So with our finite mind and limited understanding of the essence and nature of the Trinity, which is weak at best, we try and understand what Scripture says about them. In reality we are always going to be left with questions and trying to fit the Trinity into language like Father, brother, bridegroom, nurturer, comforter, etc. and this will always fall far short of the reality of their being.

But Scripture is clear about one thing – the Trinity made mankind in their image and expressed that by creating both male and female to represent them, as we see in Genesis 1:26,27 *"Then God said, "Let us make mankind in our image, in our likeness, so that they may rule over the fish in the sea and the birds in the sky, over the livestock and all the wild animals, and over all the creatures that move along the ground. ²⁷So God created mankind in his own image, in the image of God he created them; male and female he created them."*

We see in Genesis, and throughout Scripture, that man and woman share many things in common. They have a shared origin, commissioning and destiny, a shared tragedy and the same shared hope for a better future.

Shared origin

Adam and Eve were created by God and they share their origin, both in God, but also in each other. In Genesis 1 we read that God made mankind in His own image, male and female. In Gen 2:7 we read that God created the male from the dust of the earth, breathed into his nostrils the breath of life (spirit) and the male became a living being. Then later in that chapter (v 22,23) we're told how God created the female.

Gen 2:21-23, *"So the Lord God caused the man to fall into a deep sleep; and while he was sleeping, he took one of the man's ribs and then closed up the place with flesh. ²²Then the Lord God made a woman from the rib he had taken out of the man, and he brought her to the man. ²³The man said, "This is now bone of my bones and flesh of my flesh; she shall be called 'woman', for she was taken out of man."*

God made woman using the man's DNA and the man's substance. This is important because it says to us that woman was sourced in man, not something else, not something different or lesser. Woman was created from man, she was not made out of another piece of earth, which could have had a different composition to the earth the male was made from. God made them from the same stuff; they are two parts of one whole. This scriptural understanding contrasts starkly with the Greek beliefs that came through Homer and Semonides, who said that women were made from different stuff and were a different species. It also addresses the beliefs that many in the church have that woman was somehow made a lesser being than man.

Some people have made much of the fact that the woman was created second, and suggest that this gives the man superiority, and even authority over her. However, if we followed the reasoning that order of creation assured superiority and authority then, logically, the animals and stars would have authority over the man. As we will see later, women was created to stand as an equal alongside the man, with complementary abilities. She was created to be a suitable helper – not subservient, but with abilities and perspectives that he doesn't have.

One name, two people

In the beginning both male and female shared the same name – Adam – which meant mankind. It wasn't until later that Adam became the man's name and Eve became the woman's name.

Gen 5:1-2 *"This is the book of the generations of Adam. In the day* *that God created man, in the likeness of God made he him; ² Male and female created he them; and blessed them, and called <u>their</u> name Adam (Mankind), in the day when they were created." (KJV)*

In original Hebrew texts from Genesis 1 up until Genesis 3 Adam was a generic term describing both the man and the woman. It became the man's name when the woman was named Eve by the man after the fall. No longer one in identity and equality, they became two individuals who eventually forged separate, and often opposing, beliefs about their identity, role, and place in the earth.

Shared commissioning and destiny

Back in Genesis 1 we see that after God created them, He then blessed them and commissioned them both with a joint commission and mandate.

[28]"God blessed them and said to them, "Be fruitful and increase in number; fill the earth and subdue it. Rule over the fish in the sea and the birds in the sky and over every living creature that moves on the ground. [29]Then God said, "I give you every seed-bearing plant on the face of the whole earth and every tree that has fruit with seed in it. They will be yours for food. [30]And to all the beasts of the earth and all the birds in the sky and all the creatures that move along the ground—everything that has the breath of life in it—I give every green plant for food." And it was so."

God gave them joint leadership in the earth and called them to work together as a team, to work and be fruitful, multiply themselves and the fruit of the earth, and take dominion over it.

Ezer

Let's look deeper into Gen 2:18-25 at the creation of the woman who would come to be called Eve.

"[18] The Lord God said, "It is not good for the man to be alone. I will make a helper suitable for him." [19] Now the Lord God had formed out of the ground all the wild animals and all the birds in the sky. He brought them to the man to see what he would name them; and whatever the man called each living creature, that was its name. [20] So the man gave names to all the

livestock, the birds in the sky and all the wild animals. But for Adam no suitable helper was found. ²¹ So the Lord God caused the man to fall into a deep sleep; and while he was sleeping, he took one of the man's ribs and then closed up the place with flesh. ²² Then the Lord God made a woman from the rib he had taken out of the man, and he brought her to the man. ²³ The man said, "This is now bone of my bones and flesh of my flesh; she shall be called 'woman,' for she was taken out of man." ²⁴ That is why a man leaves his father and mother and is united to his wife, and they become one flesh. ²⁵ Adam and his wife were both naked, and they felt no shame."

A vital word is used here in Genesis 2 that gives a very clear idea of the purpose for which woman was created, the role she would play in Adam's life, as well as the role that God had for women to play down through the centuries. In our English versions of the Bible this word is rendered *'helper'* but the original word *'ezer'* has far stronger connotations than those we normally apply to the word helper. In most people's minds a helper is one who helps, serves, or is an actual servant. Yet, as we'll see, that is not what is meant by the word helper in Genesis.

In Genesis, and the rest of Scripture, the word *'ezer'* means – strong, powerful help being released into a situation. A couple of modern examples of that would be – someone coming to your aid when you are in danger, helping you in that situation, or when someone who is stuck in learning maths gets help from someone who has the skills that they don't, and can teach them or give them aid.

In Scripture this word *'ezer'* is most often used to describe God as our helper. For example it's used in the verse, "I will lift up my eyes to the hills from where my help comes" – referring to God Himself coming to our aid (Psa 121).

In the Old Testament *'ezer'* is used

- **2 times** in Genesis – God saying that He will make Adam a 'helper'. (Gen 2:18,20).

- **3 times** for nations that Israel appealed to for help (Isa 30:5; Ez 12:14; Dan 11:34).

- **16 times** for God as Israel's helper (Ex18:4; Deut 33:7,26, 29; Psa 20:2; 33:20; 70:5; 89:19; 115:9,10,11; 121:1,2; 124:8; 146:5; Hos 13:9) Ezer is used consistently in a military context in most of these verses – God is our helper, strength, our shield and defense.

In the Genesis 2 passage where the woman is created, God further qualifies the word *'ezer'* with the word translated into English as 'suitable', the word *'neged'* which means – suitable, a match (two who are alike), literally – as in front of him, equals, to be partners, pairs, sharedness, mutuality, one half of a polarity, eg will be to man what the north pole is to the south pole.

Put that all together and the full phrase *'ezer neged'* means – an equal of great strength, a strong helper, like God; a partner, one who stands alongside, helps us and fights on our behalf.

So when God says that He will make man a 'suitable helper' He is saying, "I will make one who is like Me, made in My image, one with great strength who will be his helper and his match, his equal."

Woman is made in the image of God, just as man is – equal in worth and value, and given complementary strengths and abilities. As women, if we do not know that this is who we were created to be, we'll buy into the enemy's lies, propagated throughout the centuries, that we are weak, inept, a lesser creature, a second-rate citizen of earth, created to be subservient to men.

What this means for women

On a personal level, as a woman your first line of defence against the enemy's attack against your life, and your hope of living a full, free life, where you can follow the call of God, is your knowledge of your identity and who you were created to be as a woman. That knowledge of who God made you to be is what will enable you to stand strong. You are not just a 'servant in a support role' (in the demeaning sense of that term). You have equality in value, standing, inheritance, authority and calling. As we've seen so far, the Trinity showed that, not only in the way woman was created but in the shared commission she was given with Adam. As you'll see as you continue reading, Jesus showed this by the way He treated women and included them in all aspects of His Kingdom. Later Paul goes on to restate this, and reinforce it, in his writings in the New Testament, one example of which is in Gal 3:28 when he says *"There is neither Jew nor Greek, there is neither slave nor free, there is no male and female, for you are all one in Christ Jesus."*

Shared tragedy, shared fall

When the tragedy of the fall of mankind happened both woman and man were hugely effected. Throughout the rest of this book we'll see how both were equally robbed and how both came under the horrific consequences of their actions.

Over the years Eve has been blamed for the fall of mankind in the garden in Eden because she ate the fruit and gave it to Adam to eat too. Was Eve solely to blame for what happened that day in the garden? When we look closely, Scripture actually tells us a far different story from the one that most people have come to believe.

In Gen 3:1-20 we see the serpent's conversation with Eve and Adam in the garden, and the things that happened as a result of that conversation. The original instruction to not eat from the tree in the centre of the garden was given to Adam before Eve was created (Gen 2:15-17). Any information that Eve had about that tree was what Adam had told her, not because God had told her.

"15 "The Lord God took the man and put him in the Garden of Eden to work it and take care of it. 16 And the Lord God commanded the man, "You are free to eat from any tree in the garden; 17 but you must not eat from the tree of the knowledge of good and evil, for when you eat from it you will certainly die."

The serpent addresses Eve and says, "Did God really say, "You must not eat from any tree in the garden?" We know from verse 6 that Adam was with her when the serpent asked the question, yet he doesn't come to her aid or say a thing; he leaves her to cope with the serpent herself. We all know what happens after that – Eve falls for the serpent's deception and she eats the fruit and shares it with Adam. Eve ate because she was deceived by the serpent, not because she was intentionally rebelling against

God; verse 13 of Genesis chapter 3 tells us that. That is important to recognise. It doesn't lessen what she did, but it does give some explanation. Neither Eve nor Adam had ever been exposed to lies or deception before, so Eve didn't recognise at first that the serpent was lying and twisting what God had said.

When God talked to them about what they had done Eve realised that she had been seduced by the serpent and deceived, and she says that she fell for that deception and ate, but instead of owning up to his part in it all Adam chose to blame Eve for his sin. James 4:17 tells us what a sin is when it says this, *"It is a sin when someone knows the right thing to do and doesn't do it."* Adam didn't take responsibility, he blamed Eve, and sadly mankind has kept doing so down through the years.

Elsewhere, Scripture confirms again that Eve succumbed to the serpent's deception.

"But I am afraid that just as Eve was deceived by the serpent's cunning, your minds may somehow be led astray from your sincere and pure devotion to Christ." 2 Cor 11:3 (NIV).

"And Adam was not the one deceived; it was the woman who was deceived and became a sinner." I Tim 2:14 (NIV).

Eve was deceived by the serpent, that cannot be denied; she has, however, been wrongly blamed by many as the sole reason for the fall of mankind, even though Adam was as involved as she was. Throughout the ages many people have transferred the blame from Eve to all women, and as a result women have been shamed, denigrated, oppressed, and even hated for what happened in the garden of Eden. Tertullian is just one example of a theologian who used Eve and her deception as a type for all women:

"And do you not know that you are (each) an Eve? The sentence of God on this sex of yours lives in this age: the guilt must of necessity live too. You are the devil's gateway: you are the unsealer of that (forbidden) tree: you are the first deserter of the divine law: you are she who persuaded him whom the devil was not valiant enough to attack. You destroyed so easily God's image, man. On account of your desert— that is, death—

even the Son of God had to die."⁵

That is the same as saying that because Cain killed Abel all men must be murderers. It's ludicrous. Eve has been wrongly judged and misrepresented for so many centuries, and sadly, so too have all women. My hope is that this book helps in some way to rectify that wrong.

Who God ultimately held responsible for the fall

In Rom 5:12-21 and 1 Cor 15:21,22 Paul explains that God held Adam (the man) accountable for what happened in the garden.

Rom 5 *"¹² "Therefore, just as sin entered the world through one man (the male, Adam), and death through sin, and in this way death came to all people, because all sinned—... ¹⁹ For just as through the disobedience of the one man the many were made sinners, so also through the obedience of the one man (Jesus) the many will be made righteous."*

1 Cor 15 *" ²¹ "For since death came through a man, the resurrection of the dead comes also through a man. ²² For as in Adam all die, so in Christ all will be made alive."*

While tradition has held women responsible for mankind's fall, God actually held Adam responsible. In saying that God held Adam responsible, I am not saying that Eve had no blame or no part in it; that would be wrong. She did, but she is not what history has painted her to be – a deceiver, a seducer, and the cause of all that has gone wrong in the world. They both played a part, and both Adam and Eve brought about what we know of as 'the fall of mankind'.

Cursed or not?

Tradition also says that God cursed them and the earth. Yet again tradition has the story wrong. Nowhere does God curse Adam and Eve, but He does curse the serpent.

After cursing the serpent God then went on to tell Adam and Eve how their actions would change their lives. Their actions would have consequences, as all actions do. What they had done would forever change not only their relationship with God, but the earth as well. All of creation fell in that moment, not just Adam and Eve. Their actions would affect everyone and everything that followed after them down through the centuries.

Instead of pain free childbirth women would now bear children in pain, and on top of that she would 'desire' her husband but he would instead rule over her. That word 'desire' has connotations of 'being in competition with someone, to try and gain the upper hand' but she would lose. Adam was told that his forcefulness and strength would gain him the upper hand in that battle. Man and woman would forever be at odds with each other, each trying to gain the upper hand, but man would be stronger and force his rule on woman.

God told Adam that the ground would also come under a curse because of Adam and Eve's actions. The word curse here means an affliction, or devastating effect; their actions caused the land to be afflicted with something. Instead of being pure, pristine and super-productive, it would now produce thistles and thorns, and it would be hard work to get it to produce well. Man would now have to work hard his whole life.

Separated identities

It was at this stage that the man's and the woman's identity as one was fractured, and they became two separate identities, pulling against each other instead of working as a team. Adam started to assert dominion over the woman from this moment by re-naming her Eve. The words 'called' and 'name' in this verse have connotations of proclaiming someone as something particular, giving them a mark of individuality. No longer one, they were now two definite separated identities. When the woman was created, Adam had named her Ishshah (woman). That name had definite connotations of their shared identity and meant 'Woman or female' (opposite of man), or 'Wife' (woman married to a man). Its connotation is 'the feminine complement to his masculinity'. Now he re-names her Eve, which simply means 'life', and was a reference to her being the first woman and the one who would bear their children, becoming the mother of mankind. In re-naming her, Adam was re-defining her and straight-away began to assert dominion over her through his fallen ego. The IVP Bible background says this of Adam's naming of Eve: *"This was a demonstration of his authority... In the ancient world when one king placed a vassal (subordinate or lesser) king on the throne, a new name would often be given to demonstrate the overlord's dominion".* From that time on Adam kept the name God had given them both as his own name, and in doing so removed Eve from her shared identity with him and established himself alone as the one to bear the name that God had given them.

How important is a name, and what does it do? Why is it important to know that Adam named Eve? It's important for two reasons – it began to assert Adam's rule over the woman, but also because right from the beginning names were believed to set in place, or define, characteristics about the person being named. Even today the naming of a Jewish child is a profound and spiritual moment. Scholars through the ages have believed that naming a baby is a statement of her/his character, importance, individuality, and path in life.[5]

Shared hope

While they shared a tragic fall, God didn't leave them without hope. He already had made provision. In Gen 3:15 we see God declare that one of their descendants would crush the serpent's head. What hope that must have given them! God was not discarding mankind; He had a plan.

Jesus came to mankind (both male and female) to restore us all back to relationship with the Godhead. Through His death and resurrection Jesus triumphed over the serpent, Satan, forever removing his authority in the earth (which Adam and Eve gave to him), and giving it back to the sons and daughters of God. Mankind was once again restored to full relationship with the Trinity and was given a restored mandate to steward and rule in the earth. We have been reconciled back to God!

"...[20]Through him to reconcile to himself all things, whether things on earth or things in heaven, by making peace through his blood, shed on the cross. [21]Once you were alienated from God and were enemies in your minds because of your evil behaviour. [22]But now he has reconciled you by Christ's physical body through death to present you holy in his sight, without blemish and free from accusation." Col 1:20-22.

And we are called to be ministers of reconciliation.
"[18]All this is from God, who reconciled us to himself through Christ and

gave us the ministry of reconciliation: [19]that God was reconciling the world to himself in Christ, not counting people's sins against them. And he has committed to us the message of reconciliation. [20]We are therefore Christ's ambassadors, as though God were making his appeal through us. We implore you on Christ's behalf: Be reconciled to God. [21]God made him who had no sin to be sin for us, so that in him we might become the righteousness of God." 2 Cor 5:18–21.

Dealing with bomb damage

As I shared at the beginning of this chapter, the understanding contained here might be for you as it was for me, like a bomb going off that both destroys and brings peace. In John 8:32 we read, *"You shall know the truth, and the truth shall set you free."* In reading the information presented in this chapter you may feel it has challenged or even destroyed some of your foundational beliefs. You may feel threatened because your beliefs have been challenged and you may even feel angry that you were not told the truth.

These are normal feelings when the foundations you've built your life on are challenged, but please recognise this – our pastors today have not set out to deceive us, most of them are simply teaching what they have been taught. When I was a pastor I believed and taught the traditional church viewpoint, until I did my own study. Sadly, many of us – many pastors before us, many pastors today, and probably you – never thought to check out for ourselves whether what we were being taught was actually what Scripture says. You may even be questioning whether what I've said is truth, and that's okay.

But don't seek to put the blame on anyone – the early church leaders, our modern pastors, or even yourself – that will not help things. Instead recognise that God is bringing light and truth into your life. Do the research for yourself, check out if what I'm saying is the truth; allow God to heal the hurts, and finally, adjust how you live in light of the new truth you now have.

Strong by design

As we've seen God created women strong by design. We were created to carry and express the reality of who God is and what God is like, in this earth alongside men. We were created to stand side by side with man, equal in worth and dominion, given the same mandate to multiply ourselves both naturally and spiritually, to co-steward and have co-dominion in the earth, to be blessed and to be a blessing.

- Is it actually important to look at this subject, and if so, why?

- What relevance does this subject have to your life personally? . . . to your church? ...to Christianity as a whole?

- In regards to the Trinity – how has the traditional view of three male figures as the Trinity affected how you've seen women, if it has affected it at all?

- Does the fact that the Jewish culture has always understood Holy Spirit to have feminine characteristics change how you understand the Trinity?

- Is the idea of created hierarchy – that is Adam having greater authority because he was created first – valid? Think through the following... Adam as one name yet two people, their shared commissioning, their assignment and authority – all given them by God, How has this understanding changed your idea of the hierarchy of mankind, if at all?

- Did God curse Adam and Eve? How is this valid to understanding what happened during and after their conversation with Him?

- Did God consign women to being under man's authority?

• Did God leave men and women without hope?

• How has the information shared in this chapter affected you personally?

If using this as a group study set next week's assignment – to read chapter 3, 'Consequences of the Fall' – and think through the questions at the end of the chapter. Remember also to pray for the group or any individuals that need to be ministered to before finishing for the night.

• • • ● • • •

References

1. https://www.hebrew4christians.com/Names_of_G-d/El/el.html

2. Genesis 17:1; 28:3; 35:11; 43:14; 48:3; 49:25;

3. http://www.scielo.org.za/scielo.php?script=sci_artte t&pid=S0259-94222016000100026

4. Tertullian, *On the Apparel of Women*, Book 1, chapter 1

5. https://hts.org.za/index.php/hts/article/view/3225/7763

6. see Talmud – Brachot 7b; Arizal – Sha'ar HaGilgulim 24b

3
Consequences of The Fall

These next two chapters deal with what the fall did to men and women's relationship with each other, and therefore to society as a whole over the centuries. From chapter five onwards we look at Jesus, Paul, and the Scriptures that were a part of establishing the church's views on women, and how that has affected us in the church today.

When the fall of mankind happened both man and woman lost some things and came under some afflictions and bondages which played out through the ages up until our current time. I want to list some of these below and then look at some of them in a deeper way.

- They lost truth. Mankind lost the truth about themselves and about God.

- They lost trust – in God, and in each other.

- They lost their true identity.

- They lost their innocence and their state of glory.

- They lost security.

- They lost respect for each other.

- They lost humility.

- They would come to believe that God had cursed them.

- They would come to believe that God was abandoning them.

- They would adopt orphan thinking and beliefs.

- They would come to believe that women had been made subject to men by God

- They would come under bondage to their ego and to pride.

- They would battle with the desire for power over each other.

I know that there were more things that happened in the fall, such as sickness being released, the earth itself being afflicted with dis-ease and brokenness, and more. But the things in the list above are what I believe apply to the subject of this book, and I want to explore a little in this chapter how they played out in both personal and societal life.

What I am looking at here in this chapter is the overarching patterns and practices that have been formed in society in general, and they may not be true of every individual who has lived. There are, of course, many men and women who have lived from the knowledge that men and women are equals and have lived their lives in a way that showed that. They have treated each other with dignity and respect, and have retained, or regained their sense of true identity, but sadly that does not apply to everyone, as history shows us.

They lost the truth

Adam and Eve, and subsequently all of mankind, lost so much of truth in the fall. That loss of truth has plagued us, and the beliefs and behaviours that became established as a result of it all formed much of society as we know it. Even what we believe about truth has changed from truth being 'truth' to truth being 'relative', and now to 'your truth' being what you live by.

Some of the truths they lost were –

They lost the truth about God. They came to believe that God couldn't truly be trusted, that He had secret agendas and motives in the things He did, and that He didn't have their best interests at heart. They came to believe that God was judging them harshly, was cruel and uncaring, and more…. Much of mankind still believes this about God.

They lost the truth about their identity. They lost their innocent and unimpaired knowledge of who they were as people created in the image of God, and in doing so lost their true sense of identity. They were deceived into thinking that they were not like God but could become like Him if they did certain things. Because they fell for that deception and lie they then saw God, themselves, and each other differently, and adopted what I call 'orphan thinking'. To me orphan thinking is sourced in the feeling of being separated from God and each other – feeling abandoned and alone and like you have to fend for yourself. When Christ came He re-established the truth concerning our identity, showing us how to live as children of God.

They lost the truth of what actually happened when God confronted them. The truth got distorted and they came to believe lies about what happened, seeing it from an inaccurate perspective. They came to believe that God had now become their judge instead of being their loving creator, source and father, and that they were separated from His love. Over time mankind came to believe that God had cursed them and was now extremely angry with them.

They lost the truth that they were still welcome in God's presence, and the understanding that God still wanted relationship with them. They felt excluded from God's presence, when in reality they were simply excluded from access to the garden and the two trees.

They lost the truth about each other. They lost sight of who each other truly was as a person created in God's image, with a shared responsibility and calling. They were set at war with each other, doubting each other's integrity and intent, and they would more readily believe the worst of each other.

Women lost the truth about themselves as much as they lost the truth about men, and came to believe that they were fundamentally flawed, less than men, as well as being created and cursed by God to be subservient to men. Overall women came to believe that most men weren't to be trusted, that they were oppressors, and more. Sadly many of these beliefs came from the way that men treated women.

Men would come to believe the lie that women were subservient to them on two counts. First – because Eve was created after Adam, therefore, in their mind, that made her second in importance, and secondly, that women had been made subject to men by God Himself. Their understanding became clouded and they lost the truth about who God made women to be, and God's intended place for them in His Kingdom. Because of that man would come to treat her as a second class citizen of little worth, believing that it was okay to oppress her, and that this was his right.

They lost their identity

Both man and woman lost their identity, and therefore their security, in the fall and so they had to find them in other ways. Again these are generalisations, but they have proved over time to be accurate.

Women

Women's identity and security were shattered in the fall. Over time they were told by society that they were second class citizens, servants, and that they had no rights of their own. They were seen by men as deceivers, the cause of all mankind's problems, and more. As you'll see in later chapters so many lies were believed about them and they were treated as if those lies were truth. This belief that the lies were truth became the excuse for much wrong treatment of women.

Over time women began to believe that their identity and security were found in their relationship with a man and with family. This loss of identity has caused women to have a low image of themselves over the years, as is shown in phrases like, "I'm just a housewife," "I'm just a mother," "My role is just to look after my family", etc. As society told them that they had no true worth outside their home they came to believe that their dreams and desires didn't matter. While this is what society portrayed, in all the women I have talked to over the years there is an instinctive knowing that they were born for more than just being useful to men and family. Instead women learnt to silence their voice in order to not make waves, or cause problems in their marriage or in society. This belief that their worth was to be found only in a man or family caused women to place inordinate pressure on themselves to be in a relationship and to have children. It caused the pressure on her to be the perfect wife, mother, housekeeper etc. in order to prove her worth.

How a woman looked has always been of importance throughout the centuries. Men prized beauty and began to seek out the most beautiful women – for a man to be seen with the most beautiful woman became a symbol of status and virility. Women were accepted or rejected on how they looked instead of being seen for who they were. This caused women to attach worth, value and identity to their looks. Society and women are still plagued by this false standard of worth today.

Men

Men also lost their security and identity in the fall. They became insecure in their identity, and their place in God's Kingdom, and instead they have often sought to find their identity and security in position, prestige or by using power and force. This has caused a competitiveness in regards to jobs, abilities and status. The higher a man's position in his job, the more competent he is deemed to be, and the more prestige he has.

Throughout the centuries men have believed that they have a God-given right to rule and hold power, and that women do not. Examples of this are numerous and are still found in every country around the world – in the church, as well as in secular society.

- **In the home, and society in general** – men have believed that women were placed under their rule and were there to do whatever their husband or other men demanded of them.

- **In government** – up until the early 1900s, politics were still viewed almost exclusively as the domain of men around the world. Even today only 24.3 per cent of all national parliamentarians were women, as of February 2019 – a slow increase from 11.3 per cent in 1995 .[1]

- **In business** – workplace inequality is still something that we are trying to correct worldwide. For centuries women were denied access to jobs outside their home, or if they did have them, they were jobs with little responsibility, and they were often given roles serving men. Women are still often paid less than men, even though they may be just as qualified and do the same job.

- **As warriors** – for many centuries women were seen as not being strong enough to fight, and were excluded from armies and positions involving strategic planning for battle etc. Yet, all throughout history women have proved that they are just as capable in this arena as men e.g. Deborah in the Old Testament, Joan of Arc, Queen Boadicea and more. And, as we've seen, God's original plan for woman was to be a strong help to man and to stand beside him with equal responsibility in the fight to protect both family and society.

- **As provider** – for many centuries men were known as the provider for their family, the hunter etc. Yet even in Scripture we see many women who did these things also – the Proverbs 31 woman is an example; she provided for her household, bought and sold land, and more. Throughout the ages women have proved themselves to be capable providers for their families.

- **Societal life** – the building industry, law, local government, medicine, science, etc. Time and time again throughout the years men have sought to deny women positions of responsibility and power in these areas because they did not believe women were capable of doing the job and sometimes also because of the perceived threat that this would be to their position, or identity, as men.

- **In church** – women up until recently have not, in most denominations, been allowed to hold positions of leadership, or to teach. They have been overlooked in ministry opportunities and not given a voice in decisions relating to church life and governance.

Men have often used position, power and force to bully women into submitting to their will in many areas of life; we'll look at that further in the next section. They used women to bolster their sense of virility, objectifying and often treating them as sexual objects to satisfy their needs.

Both men and women have needed to come back to finding their true sense of identity and security in God, and through Christ's work that has become possible.

They lost humility

Men and women lost their humility in the fall and instead began to be ruled by ego, pride and arrogance.

What is ego? The dictionary defines it as *"a person's sense of self-esteem or self-importance"* and *"the part of the mind that mediates between the conscious and the unconscious and is responsible for reality testing and a sense of personal identity."*

Richard Rohr says this about ego, *"The ego loves to take sides, and the longer and more vigorously it justifies its side, the more it feels like this is surely truth. Soon my truth easily morphs into the truth and even the only truth, we end up not with orthodoxy but with egocentricity."*

How true this has been throughout the centuries as men became convinced that they were right about their beliefs concerning women, and that they had the right to rule over them.

Megan Waterson defines it as this, *"Ego is the stories we've covered ourselves with, or the stories we have used to obscure the truth of who we really are. It's like a helicopter Mum who thinks we need protection and thinks fear will keep us safe."*

Ego is what makes us turn away from facing our questions and our fears, and seeks to make us cover ourselves with bravado and status to give us worth and confidence. It, along with pride, will even go to the extent of making us push others down to give us a sense of worth. It will do whatever is needed to keep us in what it determines is a safe place. Ego and pride are, in the end, what cause us to belittle others, to try and win the upper hand over them, to wage wars instead of making peace. It's what keeps man and woman at war with each other, and tears apart any real sense of true family. It was ego and pride that caused Adam to blame Eve instead of taking responsibility for his decision and actions.

Scripture says a lot about pride; here are just some of the verses that show what God thinks about it...

"Clothe yourselves, all of you, with humility toward one another, for "God opposes the proud but gives grace to the humble." 1 Pet 5:5

"There are six things that the Lord hates, seven that are an abomination to him: haughty eyes (pride and arrogance), a lying tongue, and hands that shed innocent blood, a heart that devises wicked plans, feet that hurry to run to evil, a lying witness who testifies falsely, and one who sows discord in a family." Prov 6:16-20 (meaning inside brackets added by me.)

"It is what comes out of you that makes you unclean. For from the inside, from your heart, come the evil ideas which lead you to do immoral things, to rob, kill, commit adultery, be greedy, and do all sorts of evil things; deceit, indecency, jealousy, slander, pride, and folly—all these evil things come from inside you and make you unclean." Mark 7:20-23.

These two things, ego and pride, also made way for arrogance to be an issue as well. The Cambridge dictionary defines arrogance as *"unpleasantly proud and behaving as if you are more important than, or know more than, other people."* Other dictionaries say things like, *"having or revealing an exaggerated sense of one's own importance or abilities." "a sense of superiority".*

In this next section I want to highlight some of the ways in which men's belief in their superiority over women has played out over the centuries in the way that they have tried to suppress women and treated them unjustly.

- For many centuries wives and daughters were seen as possessions and could be treated as such. In some places today, they still are. All women were treated as being less than a man in worth or status, often being denied what we see today as basic rights – like the right to vote, inherit, manage money, drive, and more.

- Men believed that they have the right to sexualise women or treat them as objects – Men have often used women as sexual objects in advertising. They have, and still do, often 'hit on' or mistreat a woman in a social or work situation and excuse it, thinking that it's okay.

Examples of this are too many to list fully, but include rude gestures, rude verbal expressions and names, groping, date rape, and amongst themselves as men – locker room talk and listing conquests, and more. They excuse it by saying things like, "that's just how men talk", "men have always treated women like that", "that's just the way we do things here", "she was asking for it", etc.

- In the workplace over the years men have earnt more money doing the same job as women, and in most countries they still do. We know that there are a lot of factors at play in this today, but originally it was because women weren't thought to be worth what men were worth. It's also been proven time and time again that women have often been unfairly passed over for promotions because of their gender.

- Laws in many nations still keep women in a place of being treated as a second-class citizen, and not entitled to the same rights as men – things such as the prohibition by law of women to drive cars in certain countries, the wearing of coverings from head to toe, the right to vote; many countries like Oman, Kenya and Saudi Arabia have only given women the right to vote in the last few years. In Egypt women still need their husband's, or father's, permission to leave the house. In 32 countries women still need their husband's, or father's, permission to apply for a passport.[2]

- In the church these wrong attitudes and mistreatment of women have been covered over with using Scripture as the basis and justification for their attitudes and actions. Women for many centuries have traditionally not been allowed to rise to any position of authority, to teach or to give expression to any gifts that weren't things like serving cups of tea, looking after children or doing women's ministry or missionary work. In missionary work, a lot of the time, as soon as they raised up a male capable of taking leadership they had to hand over leadership to that male.

They lost companionship and peer respect

Another of the things Adam and Eve, and subsequently all mankind, lost out on was the true companionship that could be found in each other as peers and equals. We lost respect for each other, and also lost the purity in which we originally viewed each other. Instead of being able to have relationships with the other sex that are based on mutual respect and treating each other with dignity, everything got messed up, to the point where many, including the church, came to believe that you could not have a relationship as friends and peers with the opposite sex without it becoming sexual somewhere along the line.

Over the centuries men did nothing to help this with the often deliberate sexualising and objectifying of women. So now we are left with seeing each other in ways that we were never intended to.

They lost the strength and support of each other

We've stated earlier in this book that God created women to stand alongside men, working together with them in stewarding the earth and in raising the generations that would follow them. Because of the fall we have missed the full strength of the support that we could have found in each other. Instead men and women have pulled in different directions. We have often replaced being strong willing helpers of each other with becoming strong opposing forces that had to be bent into submission by each other's will, and, if necessary, by force.

They lost trust, respect and loyalty

Both Adam and Eve sinned, but Adam also sacrificed his integrity when he didn't take responsibility for his actions and blamed Eve. This set in place a propensity within man to be willing to sacrifice his righteousness, principals and values for power, advantage and expediency. I believe this caused a loss of trust, respect and loyalty in Eve toward Adam that was carried over into future generations, as men continued to sacrifice integrity for power.

It is something beautiful when a man and woman can trust each other implicitly; when this happens respect and loyalty flow so easily. How sad it is that so many women throughout the world do not feel that they can trust and respect men, and, to be honest, because of what we've seen over the years, it's perfectly understandable. Men's track record in the way they've treated women hasn't done them any favours.

As you'll read in my personal story, this whole issue of trusting men is something that I've had to work through. In my life, time and time again, certain men forced their will on me, set out to control me, or dictate what I could or could not do, in different areas of my life, including church life.

The following are a few examples of the way that men have treated women with a lack of integrity, or blamed them unfairly –

- Much violence by men in marriages and family situations is often blamed on the woman, saying that she provoked them to it in some way, when often men made a choice to be violent, or simply didn't control themselves.

- Men will often blame their wife for their own lack of integrity and unfaithfulness in marriage, using her as an excuse in some way or another for their inability to keep their lust in check.

- In rape cases, for many centuries, a man's word was believed above a woman's. So often the man has placed the blame on the woman, saying, "she led me on", "she was asking for it because of what she was wearing", "she didn't report it straight away, so she must be lying", "she's just saying that it happened because she wants attention" etc. All the reasons listed here are actual reasons given by men to justify the rape of a woman.

- Even today in many cultures there are different standards applied to men's behaviour than to women's. In many cultures men have far more liberties than women, and have got away with behaviour that women cannot on the premise that "that's just how men are."

- In Christian churches world-wide men have blamed women, saying that they are trying to usurp men's God-given authority, and to assume positions that are not legally theirs to access. These beliefs by men have led to much unfair and biased treatment of women in churches. As a result many women don't fully trust their pastors and leaders, or other Christian men, to have their best interests at heart. Many also do not trust their leaders to be unbiased and fair when it comes to how women are treated in regards to gift use, leadership positions etc.

We all lost out

We can look at history and think that men got the better deal, and in many ways they seemed to, but in other ways they were as much in bondage as women were. Ego and pride, along with man's superior physical strength, may have helped them force their rule onto women, and they may have had more privileges, more control of the purse strings, a right to inherit, or to vote, when women could not, but oh what they gave away in order to gain that feeling of superiority and those fleeting pleasures.

As I said earlier, the things that I've looked at in this chapter are overarching patterns and practices that were formed in society in general over the centuries. Though the majority of men held society's, or the church's, view of women to some degree, there have been some men who did not, but they were few.

Go deeper

Had you ever spent time thinking about what man and woman lost in the fall? In the following areas think about the effect on Adam and Eve in what they lost, but also think about the effect it's had on your life and on the church in general through the ages.

- The loss of truth. How did losing the truth affect them? How has it affected you, and the church through the ages?

- How did losing trust in each other affect them? How has the loss of trust between man and woman affected the church through the ages? Has the loss of trust between man and woman affected you? How do you view the opposite sex?

- How was their identity affected? What type of thinking became their default thinking?

- How did losing their humility affect them? Has this had an effect in the church through the ages?

- Does orphan thinking exist? If so, can you identify how some of the ways it has been at work in mankind and in the church? What can we do about that?

- Why do we blame each other for our problems instead of owning them, facing them and dealing with them?

- What can we do to rebuild trust in each other? Is trust something that should automatically be given? Can it be demanded because of position, or is it earnt?

If using this as a group study set next week's assignment – to read chapter 4, 'Before Jesus' – and think through the questions at the end of the chapter. Remember also to pray for the group or any individuals that need to be ministered to before finishing for the night.

References

1. https://www.unwomen.org/en/what-we-do/leadership-and-political-participation/facts-and-figures Inter-Parliamentary Union. "Women in national parliaments," as of 1 February 2019.

2. https://www.thelily.com/8-restrictions-on-womens-rights-around-the-world/

4
Before Jesus

As we've just seen, after the fall the work of Satan continued and mankind got real messed up, and is still messed up today. I want to look back now at some specific cultures that played a big part in forming western society, in particular, and church culture as well.

Satan continued twisting the intent of God's words in people's hearts and over time his craftiness and deceiving nature caused many to believe his devious lies. Those beliefs that God had cursed mankind and made the woman subservient to men became the prevailing belief and caused the way that women were seen and treated to deteriorate over the centuries, until Jesus came and re-established truth.

While this was true of practically all societies, I want to concentrate on three main societies and how their view of women affected the known world, leading up to the time of Christ and beyond – Greece, Rome and Israel. By the time the Greeks and Romans appeared on the world stage, the ideas that society had about women were already entrenched, but now they would explode into a whole new level of repression and lies. Already women were believed by many to be weak, evil in intent, deceivers, and were generally treated as second class citizens with no rights; in most societies they were basically on the level of a slave. A woman could be bought or sold (the bride price was indicative of this), she usually had no say in who she was married to, she could be divorced for no reason, spoken down to, and beaten – just as any slave could. This was as true of Israel, as it was of other nations.

The Greeks

The Greek and Roman empires were the main origins of western civilisation as we know it, especially the Greek empire and its beliefs. That empire reached the peak of its glory around 500 BC and it influenced all of the 'then known world' for hundreds of years. We still feel its influence today in many of our western beliefs.

Let's look at the Greek view of women. Greek poets and philosophers had a major influence on their society. Their writings shaped how the world would see women, and they still do, even to our present times, and they became the text books that men learnt from for centuries. While this is just a brief sample of how they viewed and treated women, these views permeated all their literature, teachings, and society in general.

Some of those Greek poets and philosophers who had incredible influence were Homer, Hesiod, Semonides, Plato, and Aristotle.

Homer was the most influential author of the day and his works were to become part of the foundational belief system of all western society. In Homer's work "The Illiad" – one of the all-time Greek classics that would become a text book in their schools – the principal God Zeus abuses his wife Hera, saying to her things like, *"I shall scourge thee with stripes. Dost thou not remember when thou wast hung from on high, and from thy feet I suspended two anvils and about thy wrist cast a band of gold that could not be broken. And in the air amid the clouds thou didst hang*[1]*."*

Many times in this work Zeus abuses his wife, showing that ill-treatment and disdain of women was acceptable practice (how the gods viewed women determined how men viewed women). Homer is also quoted in the Illiad as saying, *"Be thou never gentle to thy wife"*, and in everyday life as saying, *"Do not tell your wife everything – for there is no faith in women."*

Here's some other things these men said about women. Remember, their writings were the foundation for all learning in their society:

Hesiod – *"Women are a deadly race of guile and evil, a shameless mind and a deceitful nature." "The gods declared man's punishment for sin was women!"* [2]

"The women will cause sorrow and mischief to men. They are God's punishment and curse."

Semonides – *"For Zeus designed this (woman) as the greatest of all evils and bound us to it in unbreakable fetters." "Women are a different species altogether – the gods made the mind of women a thing apart."* [3] Semonides also taught that women came from various tribes – from the long haired sow, the evil fox, from a dog, from the dust of the earth, from the sea, from the stumbling obstinate donkey, from the weasel, the monkey, and the bee.

Plato – *"The price of our sinning (as men) was exacted at the beginning of time by Zeus himself when he afflicted us with these creatures. He also designed it that we could neither exist without their aid nor bear their company. We cannot escape this pain, for it lives amongst us. It is our sisters, our mothers, our betrothed, our wives, our daughters, our mistresses and concubines. Furthermore if we spend our lives in wrongdoing and in cowardice, Zeus will send us back into this life as women." "In this fashion, then, women and the whole female sex have come into being."*[4]

Aristotle said women are *"a monstrosity", "a deformed male,"* and also said *"The female sex has a more evil disposition than the male. The male is by nature superior and the woman inferior, the male ruler and the female subject."*[5] He also declared that women were far less divine than men since only semen carried life. Aristotle, Plato and many of the Greek doctors and scientists believed that semen contained miniature fully formed human beings and that women were merely incubators and had no part in the actual reproductive process.

All these men, and many more besides them, believed and taught that the god Zeus designed women as the greatest of all evils.

Even though Greece is viewed as being the birthplace of democracy, neither women nor slaves were ever viewed as being worthy of being given democratic rights. This was the foundation of western civilisation and our knowledge about women. In hundreds of years of Greek literature there are very few favourable comments on women! The views of these men continue to influence us even today.

The Romans

The Roman view of women was no better. Roman society had part of its origins in the plundering of the people group, the Sabines[6.] They plundered their society, killed all the men, kidnapped and raped the women, and out of that came the birth of the Roman society and culture. This was re-enacted and celebrated in every marriage ceremony – the women wore veils as a symbol of mourning, the man she was being married to would strip the veil off, pick up the woman and forcibly carry her over the threshold as a symbol and re-enactment of the original Sabine conquest and a celebration of their victory. Many other Roman marriage customs are still practiced today in our modern wedding ceremonies.[7]

Their writers and philosophers openly despised women. Romulus, one of Rome's founders, in 'The Laws of the King' compelled families to rear every first born male and female child in order to continue society, but any children born after them had no legal protection from death at birth, as Roman men had the right to say whether their other children lived or died. It was generally accepted amongst society, especially the nobles, that male children would live, and whether girl children did or not was optional, the father making that decision.

Roman men had three names – individual, family and tribe. Women had no name of their own, only the clan name and the family name.[8] Instead of being given their own name they were usually known by the feminine version of their father's name e.g. Agrippa (Father) Agripina (Daughter). If there was more than one female daughter then they were named 1, 2 and 3 e.g Agripina prima, Agripina secundus, Agripina tertia, etc.

Among their gods the Romans worshipped Venus, the goddess of erotic love and the protector of prostitutes. Venus' enemy was Juno – the goddess of marriage. Venus was portrayed as gorgeous, powerful, and desirable. Juno was believed to be shrewish, insubordinate, scheming, and she was physically abused by her god husband and was powerless to prevent his infidelities. This is also how the Romans saw their women – either as objects of erotic desire, or unpleasant necessities.

They firmly believed that marriage was an inconvenience, an obligatory duty that was sadly necessary to endure, and that their wives needed to be kept firmly in their place. Many of their spokesmen encouraged men to be unfaithful to their wives, such as Ovid who said, *"This I do advise, have two mistresses; he who is stronger can have more."*[9]

They saw women as basically evil, and viewed treating them badly as giving them their just reward. Roman husbands had the right to kill their wives for either adultery or drunkenness, therefore women weren't allowed to drink wine.[10] However, if the man committed adultery, the woman had no rights to address that. A man's adultery was not only condoned, but expected, and protected by law.

Over time in Rome the lot of some women changed – as men went to war women had to take up the slack in business etc. but the fundamental beliefs of Romans never changed; any changes that did happen were mostly a matter of expediency, not belief or culture change. Women were still viewed as being possessions, the property of men, just as slaves were.

The Greek and Roman views influenced much of the then known world including Israel.

Israel

Israel was very much influenced by both Greece and Rome in many aspects of their culture over the years, as well as by the other cultures that surrounded them. Their time in Egypt as slaves had an effect on their mind-sets for many years, as did the religious beliefs of neighbouring tribes and cultures. We see this time and time again throughout Scripture as they intermarried and left worshipping God to worship other gods.

Likewise the Jews' treatment of women was influenced by all these cultures, although in many ways the Jews were harder on their women than some of the other nations. In most cultures women were regarded as the property of men and were treated as such. Israel was no different – although they varied over the centuries, sometimes treating their women better than at other times, their underlying beliefs and practices were really that women were second class citizens.

Their women were regarded as property[11] and under the authority of either their father or their husband. Even when their fathers dearly loved them this was still the case – fathers or husbands had deciding rights over their lives. They were usually denied schooling, as it was generally believed that their place was in the home and, in most cases, they had no inheritance or rights of their own.

Over years the teachings of various religious sects, such as the Pharisees and their Rabbis, were added to the Torah. Many times this happened to try and protect Jewish society from falling into the traditions and beliefs of other societies, but in fact what it did was make harsher and harsher laws that they had to obey. Many of their religious writings and teachings strayed a long way from Genesis and heaped scorn upon Eve and women in general. They often believed that women were more sinful and evil than men, more prone to fornication,[12] were gluttonous, of unstable temperament, and more. The Pharisees believed that women were a man's possession, to be used or avoided altogether. Some Pharisees even believed it was a sin to look upon a woman. They became known as 'the bleeding Pharisees' because they often ran into things while walking with their eyes shut so that they could avoid looking on a woman.

Women weren't deemed worthy of schooling or of being able to worship alongside men. By Jesus' time they were usually restricted to the women's court in the temple and they often worshipped behind screens in their synagogues, and in some cases entered by separate doors than the men did. Women were openly discouraged from reading the Torah, and the men believed that a woman would only be made unhappy by studying it. It was believed that while men could serve God, no child, slave or woman could ever serve God fully, so that meant in practice that it was a waste of a man's time to teach them. Many of the Jewish Rabbis held these views, as seen in the following recorded statements made by Rabbis[13].

"It would be better to see the Torah [the laws of God in Scripture] burnt than to hear its words upon the lips of women."

"Teaching a girl is the same as starting her on the road to depravity."

The Jerusalem Talmud states *"Let the words of Torah be burned up, but let them not be delivered to women."*[14] Viewpoints such as this were common throughout the centuries in Jewish society.

There were others, however, who viewed women as God did and tried to remind Israel that God declared His creation good, and that women were included in that declaration, but they were few and far between.

There were women in Israeli society who rose above the norms of society to follow God's calling on their life, or do other amazing things, such as Deborah who became a prophet and judge of the nation and who went into battle alongside Barak. Others like Miriam, Huldah and Anna also became prophetesses and served the Lord and the people of Israel.

In 1 Chron 7:24 we see reference to Sheerah (Ephraim's daughter and Joseph's granddaughter). This woman is recorded in Scripture as having built lower and upper Beth-horon, and Uzzen-sheerah. Not only was she responsible for the building of three towns, but two of them are still standing today because the foundations were built so well. To do this she had to have some understanding of things like leadership, management, town planning, fundraising, budgets, civil engineering, etc.

Sadly these women were the exception to society's norms.

The Daughters' inheritance

As I said earlier, women in Israel had no right of inheritance. In three separate instances in the Old Testament God speaks into this inequality and injustice when women sought, and gained, an inheritance that normally was only reserved for men.

In Num 27:4 we see Zelophehad's daughters go to Moses after their father's death to make a request of him and God. *"Why should the name of our father be withdrawn from among his family because he had no son? Give us a possession among our father's brothers."*

Moses took their request seriously and sought God about it and God had a surprising reply, which was to carry the same force as law: *"So Moses brought their case before the Lord, ⁶ and the Lord said to him, ⁷ "What Zelophehad's daughters are saying is right. You must certainly give them property as an inheritance among their father's relatives and give their father's inheritance to them. ⁸ "Say to the Israelites, 'If a man dies and leaves no son, give his inheritance to his daughter. ⁹ If he has no daughter, give his inheritance to his brothers. ¹⁰ If he has no brothers, give his inheritance to his father's brothers. ¹¹ If his father had no brothers, give his inheritance to the nearest relative in his clan, that he may possess it. This is to have the force of law for the Israelites, as the Lord commanded Moses.'"* (Num. 27:5-11).

In that moment God contradicted centuries of prejudice and man-made tradition. He made it clear that in His Kingdom, women are not afterthoughts or appendages. They have equal value with men and full rights to inherit in His Kingdom.

Later Caleb's daughter Achsah would also get a fruitful inheritance (Josh 15:19), as well as Job's daughters Jemimah, Keziah and Keren-happuch, (Job 42:12-15).

In all these instances the Trinity were at work showing us their heart for women, but many of the men of Israel did not pick up on it. Jesus, and later Paul, picked up on this discrepancy – they openly recognised, and gave women back, their rightful place in God's Kingdom and on earth. This is the foundation of society as we know it, and these basic foundational beliefs were never really recognised and challenged until Christ and Paul came along.

Go Deeper

- Hesiod's statement, "Women are a deadly race of guile and evil, a shameless mind and a deceitful nature" expressed sentiments that were believed and echoed by many in society (before Jesus and afterwards). Think about how statements like that from national thought-leaders can influence a society into believing certain people or races are second-class. What generalisations or prejudicial statements about women (or men), that aren't actually true, have you believed?

- How has prejudice and sexism affected your life? Have you found yourself believing generalisations and lies about women or men? Have you repeated them yourself?

- Think about a statement that has been used to "put you in your place as a woman" or that you have used to put a woman "in her place". Is there anyone that you need to get in touch with, apologise to, and ask forgiveness of in regards to that?

- Have sexist statements been levelled against you personally? Have you processed them through with the Lord, allowed Him to heal your woundedness, and forgiven those who mistreated you?

- In regards to the Israelite view of women, did that surprise you? What was it that surprised you?

If using this as a group study set next week's assignment – to read chapter 5, 'Jesus – Back to the Original Plan' – and think through the questions at the end of the chapter. Remember also to pray for the group or any individuals that need to be ministered to before finishing for the night.

References

1. Homer, The Iliad, Volume 1 Harvard University Press 1965. 8.161-166

2. Hesiod, The Theoginy in Hesiod. Harvard University Press 1936. 507–616

3. Semonides, Fragments from Semonides quoted in Sarah Pomeroy's book "Goddesses, Whores, Wives and Slaves". Schoken Books 1975. 49–52

4. Plato, Timaeus in Plato, Volume VII. Harvard University Press 1941.91 a–d

5. Aristotle, Aristotle Volume XIII, The Generation of Animals, and Physiognomics in Aristotle XIII, Harvard University Press 1963. 4.3 (767b 4–8)

6. https://www.ancient-origins.net/news-history/rape-sabine-women-002636

7. https://www.explore-italian-culture.com/ancient-roman-marriage.html https://rome mrdonn.org/weddings.html

8. Titus Livy, From the Founding of the City, Books I & III, Harvard University Press 1939. 1.4.1–9

9. Numa Denis Fustal De Coulanges, The Ancient City, Doubleday Anchor Books 1882. 42–43

10. Dionysious of Halicarnassus, The Roman Antiquities Volume VII, Harvard University Press 1950. 2.25.4–7

11. Sharon Hogdin Gritz, Paul, Women Teachers and the Mother Goddess at Ephesus, University Press of America 1991.

12. Testament of Reuben 5:1-5 quoted in David Scholers "Womans Adornment" 1980. Daughters of Sarah, 6.1(January – February 1980). 4.

13. Bristow, John Temple, What Paul Really Said About Women, (HarperCollinsPublishers,1988. 21

14. J. Sotah 19a. Quoted by Richard N Longnecker in "Women, Authority, and the Bible, Intervasity Press 1986. 70

5
Jesus – Back to the Original Plan

God challenges the ruling beliefs

Throughout His life and ministry Jesus honoured women, treated them with love and respect, and gave them equal place to follow Him, learn from Him and be commissioned by Him, giving them assignments of equal weight with men that would further His Kingdom in the earth. He stood up to the cultural and religious beliefs of the day concerning women and openly repudiated them in his life and ministry by including women in all He did. Jesus was, in fact, a true feminist by the definition of the word; one who believes in the equality of women (social, legal and political)[1].

I love how even Jesus' conception and birth challenged some of the ruling beliefs of society in that time. In Greek mythology and religious belief, the goddess Athena was born without the aid of a woman from the brain of Zeus (she grew fully formed in his head)[2] and woman had no part in her birth at all. Because of that she was considered worthy of worship. Out of that story, and in their general ignorance in those days of how the human body worked, came the belief that women had no part at all in the reproductive process, but were merely incubators. But in Jesus' conception and birth God did something that challenged that – when Christ was conceived and born without the aid of a male.

Jesus' life and ministry

Once I recognised God's original plan for women I was able to see how radical and inclusive Jesus was; I had always loved Jesus, but the more I saw how He treated women the more I respected Him.

In Jesus' day it was customary for the teacher to sit on low cushions or chairs as they taught their disciples. The disciples would sit on the ground below or around them and this was known as "sitting at their feet". It was the customary place of learning for a disciple. In Acts 22:3 Paul describes himself as one who learnt "at the feet of Gamaliel".

Jesus' permanent companions and followers included many women who travelled with Him, learnt from Him, and also helped support His ministry financially (Luke 8:1-3). Women learnt from Him as disciples – something that had been denied them for centuries. For example, Mary was one such woman who sat at His feet to learn in the culturally recognised mentor / pupil, or rabbi / follower, position of learning, showing that she was an accepted disciple of Jesus (Luke 10:38,39).

"*38 As Jesus and his disciples were on their way, he came to a village where a woman named Martha opened her home to him. 39 She had a sister called Mary, who sat at the Lord's feet listening to what he said.*"

Jesus honoured women and treated them as equals in all His dealings with them. Luke 13 is a passage that demonstrates this equal treatment and is a wonderful example of His restoration of women to their rightful place. Here Jesus calls a woman over and heals her, but he does more than that. All those present would have known by what He said that this was about more than just Jesus healing someone. He was making a statement that she had the right to be seen as an equal. He called her 'daughter of Abraham', a term that put her on an equal place with men. At that time only men could be sons of Abraham and inherit spiritual blessing. Jesus was, in effect, saying, "There is no exclusion for women, they can inherit spiritually the same as men."

The Rabbis of the time openly taught that men should not discuss things of Scripture with their wives and daughters, and should definitely not teach their daughters.

Jesus treated women with kindness and respect – the woman caught in adultery, the Samaritan woman, the sisters Martha and Mary, the woman who anointed His feet, and many more besides them. Time and time again throughout His ministry we see Jesus challenge the Pharisees' views on women, and Jewish society's views as well. He reminded them of how Adam and Eve were created, in His teaching about divorce, where He challenged their double standard that allowed husbands to divorce wives but not wives to divorce husbands, in His treatment of the woman caught in adultery, in teaching women and men together, in calling women daughters of Abraham, and in many other situations.

When Lazarus died we see Martha receiving the same revelation as Peter did when she says, *"I believe that you are the Messiah, the Son of God, who is to come into the world."* (John 11:27). Wow, women could receive the exact same revelations as men – they had equal right to revelation!

Because Jesus was God ("I and the father are one." John 10:30), and had made us male and female in His image, He knew what it was to identify with both male and female. He was deliberate in His treatment of women, in His speech *to* them, and *about* them. Everything He did was designed to break down the walls of division and restore equality, to show that they were created in God's image.

The woman at the well

In John 4 Jesus had His longest recorded conversation with anyone in Scripture. We are all familiar with the passage in John 4:3-42 where Jesus, on His way to Galilee, stopped at the village of Sychar. There He sat down on Jacob's well while His disciples went to buy food. That break in their journey prompted an encounter with an unnamed Samaritan woman that would be recorded in Scripture and memorialised forever as the story of the woman at the well.

We enter the story at this scene – Jesus sits on the edge of the well, waiting while His disciples go to get food, and along comes a woman to draw water. Many have speculated as to why she was there at this time of day to draw water but Scripture doesn't tell us specifically; it just records Jesus's encounter with her and the effect that had on her. During their conversation Jesus has a word of knowledge concerning her life that is the beginning of a transformative process that leads her into a life she probably would never have dreamed of.

We aren't told the name of this woman in Scripture, or what happened after she led many in her village to the Lord, so we assume some things

– mostly we assume that after this encounter she faded back into a life of obscurity, but nothing could be further from the truth. In historical records of the day we see that this woman, who is unnamed in Scripture, went on to become one of the most influential evangelists and apostles of the early church. Her name was as well known by the early church as the names of the original twelve male apostles, and even today she is revered and honoured in her home town.

While we aren't told her name before the encounter, after her encounter she was baptised and she took a new name, Photini[3], meaning 'enlightened one' or 'luminous one' – from the word 'light'.

Revealing the rest of her story

Photini's encounter with Jesus impacted her to such a degree that she went from being a woman with a somewhat dubious history, to immediately going and telling everyone she could of her encounter with the Light of the World, the Living Water, Jesus. Straight away after her encounter with Jesus she witnessed to her town and many of them became believers in Christ that day and in the days ahead. The transformation in her was immediate and life-changing, altering the track of Photini's life forever, and leading her to see the lives of thousands of others changed over the years, including her family, government officials, royalty, and many more. She led her five sisters to the Lord, and also her two sons. They then became her travelling companions in sharing the gospel, going on many missionary journeys with her.

Photini went way outside the norms of society in that era. She was the first recorded Christian missionary/evangelist and was also a woman minister in a time when women were seen as having very little real value. Jesus' interaction with her thoroughly overturned that valuation, and He did so not only in this instance but in many others, too, putting women on an equal footing with men and calling women to play strategic roles in His Father's Kingdom.

In early Christian literature Photini is noted as being an apostle that was seen by the church as an equal with the original twelve, and she is still regarded this way by the Orthodox Church, who gave her the title "equal to the apostles," a special title given to some saints whose outstanding service in spreading Christianity is believed to be comparable to that of the Twelve. It has only been given to a small number of saints throughout the centuries, many of whom were women, these saints included Mary Magdalene, Thecla, Constantine, and Saint Patrick of Ireland. Some early writers and historians say that in the very early church Photini was the most well-known apostle apart from Peter, James and John, even above Paul. (In the Western Church we know more about Paul because of his writings, which got included in Scripture.)

Photini is also recognised as an evangelist whose missionary journeys took her far and wide – to Africa, Egypt, and finally to Rome to appear before Nero himself. In Rome she testified fearlessly of Jesus to Nero, led Nero's daughter Domnina to the Lord, as well as all her attendants (about 100 of them). She also led other members of Nero's family and household to the Lord, including his brother. Needless to say this enraged Nero, who determined to kill her. He immediately ordered her and her companions to be thrown into a furnace. For seven days the fire was kept burning and at the end of that time, when the furnace door was opened, Photini and her companions all emerged, unburnt and unscathed.

During her time in Rome, Photini and her companions were beaten for hours at a time with iron rods, thrown in jail, offered riches to deny Christ, and made to drink poison (which had no discernible effect on her and her travelling companions). She was later imprisoned for a time in a dry well, and from then records begin to differ. Some say she gave up her spirit and died in the well after having a visitation from Jesus; others say she was removed from the well and thrown back into a normal cell where, soon after, she had a visitation by Jesus, and after that visitation she gave up her spirit and died. Either way, Nero could not kill her; she chose the time of her departure from earth into the arms of Jesus – her last, and forever, bridegroom.

Photini is still remembered in her city, and in the Eastern Church, as being a great apostle and evangelist, a woman who radiated the life of Christ, and who won many thousands to Him. What a woman, and what a legacy she leaves for us! She has become one of my heroes of faith!

Maybe your name will never be revealed in a major best-selling book, or known by a huge portion of the church, but your life and impact will be recorded and remembered forever in the Kingdom of heaven, and you will leave a legacy behind you when you leave this life! By following the call of God on your life you make a difference, and you forge a way for other women to also be brave enough to follow their call, wherever that leads. Be you, because you are enough to make a huge difference – just like Photini did!

Women as part of Jesus' team

Luke tells us that women travelled with Jesus. They supported His ministry in many ways and learnt from Him. They were most likely there when Jesus was with the male disciples, and we know that Mary sat at His feet in a traditional rabbi / follower position for learning. While Scripture isn't explicit in saying that the women took part in the teaching times with the disciples, or were sent out on ministry, we do know that Jesus gave equal opportunity to at least two women as disciples, and as ones sent on assignment. In His doing that, we must also assume that He probably allowed the other women to learn from Him, and gave them assignments. We certainly know that in many instances when He taught, women were present, such as at the Sermon on the Mount, and in the Upper room, where the Holy Spirit was poured out on men and women alike.

Jesus commissions several women

There are no gender limits on a God given destiny and women were commissioned and sent on assignments by Jesus, as were men. One such woman was Mary Magdalene.

After His resurrection Jesus appeared to Mary and commissioned her to do an important task. He told Mary to go and tell His disciples and brothers that He had risen (Matt 28). He sent her as His ambassador! Later Mary Magdalene would become known by the early church as the Apostle to the Apostles. John and Peter had already been to the tomb, but Jesus didn't choose to reveal Himself to them. He didn't say, "Gosh, the guys aren't here, I'll have to tell a woman." He chose to send her!

In Matt 28:9-10 we read that He also told some women who came to Him that Easter morning, *"Do not be afraid. Go and tell my brothers to go to Galilee; where they will see me."*

Women reinstated!

All through Jesus' life and ministry He deliberately worked at setting right something that had been wrong for centuries, as He restored women to their rightful place as equals in every way with men.

Dorothy Sayers said this in her book 'Are Women Human? – Astute and Witty Essays on the Role of Women in Society'

"Perhaps it is no wonder that the women were first at the Cradle and last at the Cross. They had never known a man like this Man – there never has been such another. A prophet and teacher who never nagged at them, never flattered or coaxed or patronised; who never made arch jokes about them, never treated them either as "The women, God help us!" or "The ladies, God bless them!"; who rebuked without querulousness and praised without condescension; who took their questions and arguments seriously; who never mapped out their sphere for them, never urged them to be feminine or jeered at them for being female; who had no axe to grind and no uneasy male dignity to defend; who took them as he found them and was completely unself-conscious. There is no act, no sermon, no parable in the whole Gospel that borrows its pungency from female perversity; nobody could possibly guess from the words and deeds of Jesus that there was anything "funny" about woman's nature."

Jesus reinstated women to their pre-fall status as equals in value and calling. He levelled the playing field; no one else treated women like He did. In Him there was no double standard.

As a woman, seeing how Jesus treated women, taught them, and commissioned them gave me great hope and understanding – that I as a woman could learn from Him, be His disciple, and most definitely be called by God to be an ambassador of reconciliation and hope. And yes, I could even be a prophet and leader in the church!

Go Deeper

- In what ways was Jesus's treatment of women radically different from society in general?

- If Jesus is the image of the Father, and if He only did what He saw the Father doing, then what does Jesus's treatment of women say about how the Trinity view women?

- How do you think the women of that day felt to be accepted and included by Jesus?

- Photini, Mary the mother of Jesus, Mary Magdalene, Martha, Joanna, Susanna – these were all women followers of Jesus, and were amongst those He trusted, disciple and commissioned. If Jesus trusted and commissioned women, what is it that stops many churches from allowing women to minister or hold leadership positions?

If using this as a group study set next week's assignment – to read chapter 6, 'The Early Church' and Chapter 7 'Pauls Tricky Verses'– and think through the questions at the end of the chapters. Remember also to pray for the group or any individuals that need to be ministered to before finishing for the night.

• • • ● • • •

References

1. Washington Herald 1915 - https://www.bustle.com/articles/129886-what-does-feminism-mean-a-brief-history-of-the-word-from-its-beginnings-all-the-way

2. https://greekgodsandgoddesses.net/goddesses/athena/

3. Some of the sources on Photini include -

    - https://www.cbeinternational.org/resources/article/mutuality samaritan-sinner-celebrated-saint-story-first-christian-missionary

    - https://www.youtube.com/watch?v=hQYrLAmvlos

    - https://www.cbeinternational.org/resources/article/mutuality samaritan-sinner-celebrated-saint-story-first-christian-missionary

    - https://ishshahsstory.com/2016/11/02/finding-photini-light-on-the woman-at-the-well/

6
The Early Church

The very early church

Most of what we know about history relies heavily on written records, most of which were written by men, and discovering reliable historical information about Christian women can be hard. It appears from early writings that women made up a large portion of those who got saved and joined the church.

From the records that remain today and from Scripture itself we can see that leadership in the early church was shared among male and female members according to their "gifts" and talents. Women in leadership were a normal, and accepted, part of church life in the very early days of the Church. The early church continued to follow Jesus' example and women were accepted in all roles as leaders, deacons, evangelists, prophets, pastors, teachers, and even apostles.

There are many women leaders mentioned in the New Testament, such as Priscilla, Lydia, Phoebe, Euodia and Syntyche, Junia, Nympha, several Mary's, Photini, and more, and Paul is the one who mentions most of them, calling them his fellow workers, leaders, deacons, teachers and apostles. Women served as deacons, apostles, evangelists, pastors and many went on missionary journeys and established churches in other nations. Women with financial means like Lydia of Philippi acted as financiers and supported the apostles in their work.

In the 2nd century, Clement of Alexandria wrote that the apostles were accompanied on their missionary journeys by women who were not marriage partners, but colleagues, *"that they might be their fellow ministers in dealing with housewives. It was through them that the Lord's teaching penetrated also the women's quarters without any scandal being aroused. We also know the directions about women deacons which are given by the noble Paul in his letter to Timothy."*

Thecla is a woman of note from the early church, a friend and fellow minister with Paul who teaches, preaches, heals and baptizes. In the 300s both Gregory of Nazianzus and Basil of Caesarea spoke of Thecla and described her teaching centre and hospital near Seleucia. The pilgrim Egeria visited this facility in 399 A.D., and also described its monasteries, convents and assembly buildings, along with the teaching and healing ministries that went on there. The German team that excavated the center in 1908 found the apse still standing above the ground, with the main basilica's outlines covering a space equal to that of a football field. The excavators also found numerous cisterns, apparently for washing the sick, two other churches, and many fine mosaics. Centuries after her death the hospital and training centre she started continued to help many. It was in active use for at least 1,000 years.[1] That's some enduring work and legacy – what a leader she must have been!

Geoffrey Blainey notes in his book "A Short History of Christianity" that by around AD300, women had become so influential in the affairs of the church that the pagan philosopher Porphyry *"complained that Christianity had suffered because of them"*.[2]

Enter Paul

As we've seen, Paul called these women fellow workers, leaders, teachers, deacons and apostles, so where did we ever get the idea that he was against women teaching or being in ministry? That misguided idea comes from a few isolated verses that were misunderstood or mistranslated in the very early Bibles, and some of those mistranslations have yet to be corrected.

When they translated our early Bibles they translated them according to their understanding of words used, and the culture of the day, but in a lot of cases they were at least a few centuries removed from the actual time that these words were used. The meaning of many words had changed and evolved with time. The Hebrew, Aramaic and Greek versions of the Scriptures got translated into Latin and most of our Bibles up until recently were a translation into English of a Latin translation called the Latin Vulgate. Then those first translations were copied by hand by many others. Those copying the first translations didn't always have access to the original scrolls and letters. Some of them worked from church sanctioned translations – some of which had a definite bias, and others which were just badly translated through misunderstanding the Jewish culture and the original meanings of words at the time the letters were written. Also certain Emperors or Kings introduced rules to the translation process at the time translations were made that caused definite mistranslations and biases to happen.

In the last few centuries, however, more and more people have had access to the originals, due to them being made available in either print/book form or on the internet.

Many people have read our English versions of Scripture and concluded that when Paul came along he preached against women teaching and being in leadership positions, but nothing could be further from the truth. Before meeting Christ, Paul was a Pharisee, one steeped in the law and all the stuff that had been added to the original law as well. He thought like a theologian and lawyer and was a stickler for detail, as well as being a passionate defender of what he believed to be truth. Paul had very strong, traditional, pharisaic Jewish views on women and their place in society. Paul, as a Pharisee before his conversion, would have proudly prayed a prayer known today as the three blessings, thanking God that he was neither a Gentile, a slave, nor a woman[1]. This prayer is also echoed in the teachings of others outside Jewish society. In records from the third century B.C. we find a quote attributed to Socrates that expresses gratitude for having been born human and not a brute, a man and not a woman, Greek and not barbarian. By the second century BC we see the beginning of the incorporation of thoughts like these into the Jewish morning prayers that became known as the Three Blessings[1], which all Jewish men were encouraged to pray upon waking, and many still pray today.

I understand that, in their minds, Jewish men weren't putting down Gentiles, slaves and women, they were simply thanking God that they were men . . . because Gentiles, slaves and women were not allowed to participate fully in the community of faith. Yet this prayer was often the first thing women heard come out of their husbands' mouths every morning.

Even here in the Three Blessings you have a reminder of the separation of women and their not being allowed to participate fully in the faith community and learning, and women certainly could not be leaders in the Jewish faith at that period of time. By then, in the Temple, there was a court for Gentiles and a court for women – both with restricted access into the Temple . . . giving restricted access into God's presence.

After his encounter with Christ on the Damascus road Paul underwent profound changes in his beliefs and became one of the most outspoken champions *for* women since Christ. What a heart and mind change had to happen to Paul in order for him to later say, *"There is neither Jew nor Gentile, neither slave nor free, there is no male and female, for you are all one in Christ Jesus."* Gal 3:28.

Paul worked alongside, and respected, women as leaders in the early church. Sixty percent of the women he mentions in his letters he calls colleagues or co-workers, acknowledging them as leaders, deacons, pastors, evangelists and apostles. He viewed them as being equal and interdependent, not independent of each other.

"Nevertheless, neither is man independent of woman, nor woman independent of man, in the Lord. ¹²For as woman came from man, even so man also comes through woman; but all things are from God." I Cor 11:11-12.

Go Deeper

- Think about (and discuss) how the use of women as leaders in the early church would have been revolutionary, and what differences it would have meant for women as part of the early church.

- As we know the meaning of words can change over time in different societies, you only have to think of our time and the amount of words that have changed meaning in the last century – words like 'gay' which once meant 'happy'. 'Prude' used to mean "wise and good woman' or 'wise and good man' but now is used to describe someone who is 'uptight and restricted in emotion or behaviour'. How do you think the distance in time could have affected how translators viewed words they were translating in the Bible? Talk about the difficulties they would have had or the possible confusion – and who got to decide what a word meant?

This chapter and the next are part of Week 6's meeting. Read both chapters and think through the questions at the end of the chapter. Remember also to pray for the group or any individuals that need to be ministered to before finishing for the night.

● ● ● ● ● ● ●

References

1. Thecla - https://christianhistoryinstitute.org/magazine/article/women-in-the-early-church

2. Blainey, Geoffrey (2011). A Short History of Christianity. Maryland: Rowman and Littlefield. p. 43.

7
Paul's Tricky Verses

How do we view the Scriptures in our English Bibles that appear to say that Paul believed that women should not teach or hold leadership positions? What do Paul's tricky verses actually say?

When it comes to looking at Paul's writings regarding women we must read and understand them in the context of everything else that Scripture says on that subject; that must include looking at God's original plan for man and woman, as stated in Genesis.

In theology there is something known as the 'law of first mention'. This establishes the way that you look at that subject throughout the rest of Scripture, so to understand Paul's writings we must go back to the beginning and see what the 'first mentions' are in Scripture in relation to a woman's role and place in society and marriage. To fail to do this opens us to gross misunderstanding of the things we read, and sadly that is what has happened over the centuries. People have read Scripture passages in isolation from the rest of Scripture and come to conclusions as to what they mean, and as a result those conclusions have often been incorrect.

We've already established that in the beginning, when God created man and woman, He created them with equal worth, and gave them a mandate to steward and have dominion in the earth as a team. Neither was given a ruling voice, or vote, over the other. As a result of that fall, however, some things changed and God shared with them the consequences of what they had done in their act of disobedience and lack of trust. One of the consequences was that now man would seek to rule over woman.

We also need to understand some things about how the Scriptures, and Paul's letters, were written. They were not written to us today; they were written many hundreds of years ago about, and to, specific people and, in Paul's case, also to specific churches, addressing very specific situations within those churches. Many of Paul's letters are replies to questions they asked him in their letters to him.

Not everything that was written to address a specific situation can be applied universally to the church as a whole. We can learn from it but we must not make it our law. Only when we understand what was situational and what was universal can we make a decision about what applies to us, here today. To take everything that Paul wrote and say that it was written for us today is a wrong understanding of who Paul was writing to, and it is bad scholarship and an unwise stewarding of Scripture.

1 Corinthians 14

1st Corinthians is one of the letters Paul wrote in which he answered questions that had been asked of him by the Corinthian church leaders. In this letter he covers a number of different issues related to both church life and doctrine. He addresses the topics of divisions and quarrels, sexual immorality, lawsuits among believers, marriage and singleness, freedom in Christ, order in worship, the significance of the Lord's Supper, the right use of spiritual gifts, and he also included a teaching on the resurrection. In all the subjects Paul covers in this letter there is a common theme – Paul's emphasis on Christian conduct in the local church. He expected that Christian people would live according to Christ's example and teaching. Or, as he told them, *"You have been bought with a price: therefore glorify God in your body"* (6:20).

In 1st Corinthians 14 we see Paul addressing specific issues that had developed within the Corinthian church. They were behaving like those of other religions, and their meetings had descended into being a place of disorder, where everyone did what was right in their own eyes. Women chatted loudly amongst themselves on their side of the church, tongues speakers brought messages with no interpretation, and prophets tried to all speak at once and out-prophesy each other. So they reached out to Paul for help and Paul writes and answers their questions and gives them some foundational teaching so that order would be established. His goal in this letter is not to shut people down but to give guidelines to a church where they were sorely needed, so that everyone could participate, be blessed, and be understood.

In the church in Corinth most people had come out of other religions, or idol worship, in which chaos often reigned. Many of those religions often had elements of frenzied worship, with little order, and in their gatherings everyone spoke at once, often interrupting each other to get their point across.

Anything that Paul says in this chapter about women having to be silent has to be viewed in light of what he has said elsewhere. In 1 Corinthians chapter 11, several chapters before this one, Paul acknowledges that Corinthian women prayed and prophesied aloud in church gatherings, and he didn't tell them to be silent then (1 Cor 11:5). In chapters 12 and 14 of 1 Corinthians Paul mentions several ministries, some of which involve speaking or singing, and tells all the church to eagerly desire them, but he does not exclude women from seeking them, or say that they are only for men (e.g. 1 Cor. 12:7-11, 28; 14:26). So when it comes to chapter 14 either Paul is now contradicting himself when we read "women should be silent", or there is something we are not understanding about that passage.

Let's look at the verses which state that women should be silent – verses 34, 35.

"34 "Women should remain silent in the churches. They are not allowed to speak, but must be in submission, as the law says. 35 If they want to inquire about something, they should ask their own husbands at home; for it is disgraceful for a woman to speak in the church. 36 Or did the word of God originate with you? Or are you the only people it has reached? 37 If anyone thinks they are a prophet or otherwise gifted by the Spirit, let them acknowledge that what I am writing to you is the Lord's command. 38 But if anyone ignores this, they will themselves be ignored. 39 Therefore, my brothers and sisters, be eager to prophesy, and do not forbid speaking in tongues. 40 But everything should be done in a fitting and orderly way."

One of the first things we notice in these verses is that Paul appears to be quoting the law (v34). Yet nowhere in the Jewish law does it ever forbid a woman to speak in the church or temple, or say that they should be silent. Paul was intimately acquainted with the law; he was a Pharisee, he knew that the law did not say this, yet here it makes it seem like Paul is saying that it does, when in fact further study shows that he is quoting something that he was asked in their letters to him.

In the original Greek manuscripts they didn't use things like quotation marks or punctuation so early translators often had a hard time translating or even understanding what was meant. They had to do the best job they could at the time with the understanding they had; however today we have access to many more historical documents that are able to give us a better understanding of how things were written and what they meant. So that meant, that in our English Bibles things like quotation marks and certain Greek words or symbols got left out, and these verses are some of the verses where Paul quotes something said to him. Unfortunately for us, because no quotation marks show in our English bibles, it has meant that centuries of people have read and understood these verses to mean something that they don't.

Apart from missing out quotation marks to show us when Paul is quoting someone else, another thing that is not shown in our English Bibles is found at the end of verse 35 and the beginning of verse 36 in I Corinthians 14. In the original Greek there is a symbol ἤ, which our English translators didn't translate and put into our English Bibles. This symbol ἤ is an exclamation expressing disapproval or rebuttal. Our nearest English meaning for it is something like, "No way", "Nonsense", "Rubbish". it's a word that is used to disagree strongly with the statement before it. Paul used this word, this expletive, many times throughout 1 Corinthians.[2]

It's a very important part of these verses and missing it out totally changes the way the Scripture reads. Without it the verse reads like a command from Paul. With it the verse shows that Paul is both quoting and refuting what they say. So taking quotation marks and that Greek symbol into consideration these verses actually read more accurately like this...

[35] *(You guys say that the Jewish law says)* "If they want to inquire about something, they should ask their own husbands at home; for it is disgraceful for a woman to speak in the church". [36] 'Nonsense! Did the word of God originate with you? Are you the ones God revealed His will to, and His word on this?

Another important aspect of these verses is found in the fact that Paul is saying that women were allowed to ask questions and learn. This is the first time in the New Testament apart from Jesus ministry where we see that women were encouraged to learn, were allowed to ask theological questions and could ask their husbands questions and expect to get answers. Up until now, in many cultures, including the Corinthian and Jewish religious practices, it was openly believed, and taught by many Rabbis that women shouldn't receive teaching, learn the Scriptures or receive training for anything except household duties.

Paul was not telling women that they had no right to learn or to speak, or even to teach in church; he is saying that they have the same right to learn and ask questions as much as men do. But he is also saying that they should stop talking amongst themselves during their meetings, as was their custom, and if they have questions they should ask their husbands at home. Verse 26 is the main thought for this whole chapter – take turns, listen to each other!

1 Corinthians was not written to today's church; it was written to address problems in one particular church and culture. Can we learn from what Paul wrote to the Corinthian church? Definitely! And can we find in what he wrote wisdom for corporate gatherings? Yes! But only if we actually understand what he was really saying.

Ephesians 5

In his letter to the Ephesians Paul speaks into what it means to live in Christ. Part of the letter deals with how the church, and the household, was to function under Christ.

As stated earlier, we must look at what Paul appears to be saying in the light of God's original mandate to man and woman, and also in the light of the rest of Scripture. As we've seen in Genesis, God gave man and woman equal worth, rights and mandate. They worked as a team in having dominion over their assigned domain.

Yet society had moved far from that. The church in Ephesus grew from a mixture of Jews who lived there and converts who had come from a society where they were intellectually proud, and full of occult activity and sexualised worship in their temple rituals. These people needed a good foundation laid for how different life in Christ was.

Paul lays out a whole new radical alternative to the way society and households usually ran in the cultures of the day. In Ephesians 5 we see Paul tell the Ephesians that Christian households were to be based on both parties being filled with the Spirit, submitting mutually to one another in love, and with respect. Women were to honour, respect and be devoted to their husbands. Husbands were to love like Christ loved, even being willing to lay down their lives for their wives. Both were to love each other as Christ loved them. Paul declared that God's purpose was to bring all things into unity in Christ (Eph 1:10) He declared that men and women are heirs together in Christ (Eph 2:4-10). Equal heirs – equal in being forgiven, in hope, in mandate, and in purpose (as they were in Genesis).

Wow, what a difference to women being seen as the property of men, forced to submit to whatever their husband wanted to do with them, husbands being unfaithful and often having multiple mistresses, beating their wives, treating them as servants, and being able to divorce them without just cause.

We've talked elsewhere about the law of first mention and God's first instructions about marriage. Paul refers them back to this and says that this is the basis we build on. These instructions are found in Gen 2:24 and also referred to in Matt 19:5 and Eph 5:31. These verses talk about the man leaving his father and mother, cleaving to his wife, and the two becoming one. Becoming one is more than just about sexual intimacy; it is about becoming one in heart, mind and purpose, and operating as one in all things pertaining to the marriage, including responsibility and authority. It's about being a team. These verses say that when we marry, we come out from under the authority of our parents and become accountable to our spouse. Husbands become accountable to their wives, just as wives become accountable to their husbands.

But what I've described above is not what we've traditionally been taught in our Western churches. In Ephesians 5 in our English Bibles we read some verses that appear to say that men have headship, or authority and rule, over women and that women must submit to men.

Verses 15-23 in this chapter are actually one long sentence in the Greek, with no punctuation or separations and it is all part of one idea, one point. To make it easier for people to read and understand the translators decided to break it up into sentences and put dividing headlines in as well. This meant that people began to view it as a whole pile of separate thoughts and points.

Let's look at the verses that people stumble most over, verses 21-24, and see if we can find out what they actually mean, and where we've gone so wrong. The King James Version translates it as... *21 "Submitting yourselves one to another in the fear of God. 22 Wives, submit yourselves unto your own husbands, as unto the Lord. 23 For the husband is the head of the wife, even as Christ is the head of the church: and he is the saviour of the body. 24 Therefore as the church is subject unto Christ, so let the wives be to their own husbands in everything."*

Verse 21– In this verse, where Paul says very clearly that we should all submit ourselves to one another as Christians, we need to understand what this word submit meant to Paul and to the Ephesians. This word had two main meanings in culture – one in military use, and one in normal life. In military use it meant to obey or be under obedience, like a soldier is to their commanding officer, but in non-military use it meant a voluntary attitude of cooperation and assuming responsibility, or carrying a burden. The church in Ephesus was not a military context, they were civilians, so the non-military use of the word is the one Paul meant when writing to the church in Ephesus and to the husbands and wives there. It did not mean that one person was to allow themselves to be ruled by another, or that we were to seek to rule over each other.

Verse 22 – In our modern translations this verse reads, *"Wives submit yourselves (be subject) to your own husbands as you do to the Lord."* In the original writings the words 'submit' or 'be subject' are not used at all. The original Greek version which includes verse 21 as part of the same sentence reads – *"21 "Submitting yourselves one to another in the fear of God, wives to your own husbands, as to the Lord".* It's part of the same sentence that is talking about mutual submission. What is talked about here is about two people mutually putting each other first out of love, honour, respect and mutual accountability, not of 'having to' submit. We see this brought out in several other translations.

The Contemporary English Version (CEV) says in v 22, *"A wife should put her husband first, as she does the Lord."*

The JB Phillips translation translates 'submit' in verse 22 as, *"adapt yourselves to your husbands."*

The New International Revised Version (NIRV) translates it as, *"follow the lead of your husbands as you do the Lord."*

The Orthodox Jewish Bible translates it as, *"make yourselves accountable to."*

These translations fit more in line with Paul's original intent, and what the rest of Scripture says, than does the King James Version and other versions which use the words 'submit' or 'be subject to'.

Verse 23 – In verse 23 in many of our translations we read, *"the husband is the head (kephale) of the wife as Christ is the head (kephale) of the church…"*

Over the years this verse in particular has been used to support the view that a woman should be in submission because the man is the boss, or ultimate authority, in a marriage. This word *'head'* or *'kephale'* is the word I mentioned earlier that had come to mean something quite different by the time the translators came to translate Paul's letter. When Paul wrote his letter the word *'kephale'* was commonly understood to mean *'source'* or *'point of origin'*, not authority or boss. It referred to the point of origin of something such as the headwaters, or source, of a river. Many other writings from that same time period confirm the meaning of kephale as 'source'. It wasn't until several centuries after Paul's death that some men in the church started to teach that kephale meant leader or authority. Some church leaders tried to correct the new interpretation as it started to gain momentum, but they were eventually drowned out, and *'authority'* is what the word *'head'* came to mean to the church.

Other early church leaders that confirmed the meaning 'source' for the word 'kephale' (head) were -

- Cyril, Bishop of Alexandria (AD 375-444) commenting on 1 Cor 11:3, defines the head metaphor as 'source': *"Thus we say that the* kephale *(source) of every man is Christ, because he was excellently made through him. And the* kephale *of woman is man, because she was taken from his flesh. Likewise the* kephale *of Christ is God, because he is from him according to nature."*

- Theodore, Bishop of Mopsuestia in Cilicia (AD 350-428) interprets the metaphor as 'source or origin of life'. He held that *"just as Christ was considered head of all who had been born anew in Him, so the woman has man as her head or source since she had taken her being from him."*

- John Chrysostom, Bishop Of Constantinople (AD347-407) commenting on 1 Cor 11:3 said the "head" metaphor does not mean that one has authority over another or one is under subjection to another. He wrote *"For had Paul meant to speak of rule and subjection, as thou sayest, he would not have bought forward the instance of a wife but rather of a slave and a master."*

So Paul is, in fact, saying here that man was the source from which woman came (which is, I believe, a reference back to Eve being sourced from Adam's substance), just as Christ was the point of origin of man, because He created man. If the word *'kephale'* meant *'authority'*, and every woman who has ever been a wife was placed under the authority of her husband, then every man ever born must already be under the authority or lordship of Christ; yet we don't take it to mean that.

Man as head of the home

Another meaning that the church over the centuries has applied to these verses is to say that Paul meant that the man is the 'authority' or 'head of the family', or the 'priest of the family'. Nowhere does Paul say this, and nowhere does Scripture support this teaching. It is a man-made doctrine established from this one verse, to place men in a position of superiority to their wives and children. Again we must look at what God's original plan for mankind was, and what Scripture teaches overall. If we do so we see that man and women were created equal in value and worth, given equal dominion and authority, and both are told to be mutually submissive one to another.

God promotes a marriage of equal responsibility, accountability, teamwork, honouring of each other's gifts and strengths, and using them to build a family together. They are both held responsible in God's sight for the spiritual atmosphere in the home, both responsible to see their children trained in the ways of God, and both are called to worship Him and to warfare on behalf of each other, and their family.

Verse 24 – This verse follows on from the ones above and is all part of the same section in Paul's writing. It must, therefore, be viewed through the same understanding. Again, the words *'should be subject'* concerning wives are not in the original versions of these scriptures, they are a later addition added around 300AD. And, as we've already established, the word 'subject' is about accountability not rule, so in speaking about the church being 'subject' to Christ, Paul is saying the church is accountable to Christ in all it does.

In all the verses we've looked at in Ephesians, wives are accountable to their husbands in all things, as husbands are to their wives.

Paul's letters to Timothy – 1 Timothy 2:12

In this passage we read, *"A woman should learn in quietness and full submission. I do not permit a woman to teach or to assume authority over a man; she must be quiet."*

Many have taken this to mean that no woman should have authority, or a leadership position, or be able to teach, yet we see many women in Scripture who did all of these; they prayed in public, prophesied, taught, led churches, and more. Paul himself worked alongside and commended many women leaders and women apostles as his fellow-workers for Christ, often expressing his admiration and thanks for them.

We need to look at the context of the time that they lived in and what was happening in this church. Timothy was working in the church at Ephesus and Paul's letters to him are ones filled with practical and pastoral advice about the situation there, which included heretical teachings that combined elements of Gnosticism, decadent Judaism (1:3-7) and false asceticism (4:1-5). [3] We also see unruly behaviour happening in their worship times.

Many scholars believe that Paul is not talking about every woman here, but a certain woman. Two Greek words were commonly used in the New Testament for 'be silent' (*siōpaō* and *sigaō*), but the word Paul uses here is neither of those. Instead he uses the word '*Hesuchia*', which means a state or disposition of calmness and of being settled. It does not mean be silent.

It is believed that his use of this word '*hesuchia*' suggests that there was a problem with an unruly woman in the church at Ephesus. However, Paul wasn't saying that she should be completely silent, but that she should settle down and learn in a submissive manner (the usual conduct of a good student), and that she should not teach, or try to dominate or coerce a certain man.

Other scholars suggest that the words Paul uses in this context are about women who seek to domineer or establish carnal authority over men by usurping their will.

One writer has suggested that a better translation of this verse would be, *"I do not permit a woman to privately disciple a man or domineer over a man. She must lead a life free from inordinate ambition, nor should she be unrestrained in feelings or behaviour."* [5]

There are often many conflicting opinions about certain passages, and sometimes we just don't know what the original writer actually meant. However we do know from everything else that Paul wrote that he was not opposed to women prophesying, praying, or taking a public role in worship, nor did he forbid them from leadership; in fact he commended their leadership. So we can safely assume that he was not saying that no woman could teach or assume a senior leadership position in a church.

1 Timothy 3:1-5

Can a woman be an overseer, a deacon, a pastor, a bishop? In 1 Tim 3:1-7 Paul lists the qualities of an overseer. These verses have been used for centuries to exclude women from leadership roles in the church, yet do they actually do that?

The King James Version and the New American Standard both translate this passage in a way that seems to indicate that only a man can desire to be an overseer or bishop. But is that what the original says?

"¹It is a trustworthy statement: if any man aspires to the office of overseer, it is a fine work he desires to do. ² An overseer, then, must be above reproach, the husband of one wife, temperate, prudent, respectable hospitable, able to teach,³ not addicted to wine or pugnacious, but gentle, peaceable, free from the love of money. ⁴ He must be one who manages his own household well, keeping his children under control with all dignity ⁵ but if a man does not know how to manage his own household, how will he take care of the church of God?" NASB

Here we see three statements that could lead us to believe that this is the official church position on the subject, as stated by Paul.

- "it is a trustworthy statement"

- "if any man"

- and "he"

Most people reading that would immediately think that Paul is saying, "Trust me in this, leadership is a man's role."

There is a problem here, though — nowhere in the original is the Greek word *'aner'* or *'man'* used. Instead Paul uses the gender inclusive word *'tis'*, which means *'anyone'* or *'whoever'*. Wow, does that change things, or what? Anyone can desire to be an overseer, women included!

So that means the verse actually reads, as the NIV states…

"Here is a trustworthy saying: <u>Whoever</u> aspires to be an overseer desires a noble task. ² Now the overseer is to be above reproach, faithful to his wife, temperate, self-controlled, respectable, hospitable, able to teach, ³ not given to drunkenness, not violent but gentle, not quarrelsome, not a lover of money. ⁴ He must manage his own family well and see that his children obey him, and he must do so in a manner worthy of full respect."

However, even though the NIV translates some of the verse correctly, it still leaves us with the overall impression that Paul is saying that only men can fulfil this role. That's because in verse two Paul switches from addressing the fact that anyone may aspire to this to addressing any men who might seek this role. The reason for that switch in verse 2, is that in the patriarchal society of the Greco-Roman world men could divorce, remarry, keep mistresses (the more the better), and still be regarded as respectable, even godly, but women did not have any of those rights. If we read that verse correctly what it is actually saying is that an overseer should be a one-woman man. That's why Paul included these statements in verses 2-4, because it was men who were the more promiscuous, and were actually encouraged, and allowed by law, to live disloyal, adulterous lives in that society.

2 Timothy – Paul commends godly women

In 2 Timothy Paul commends godly women for their input into Timothy's life and goes on to say to Timothy in chapter 2:2, *"And the things you have heard me say in the presence of many witnesses, entrust to reliable people who will also be qualified to teach others"* (NIV). The word 'people' in this verse is a correct translation and is gender inclusive, not exclusive. Paul is saying here – find faithful men and women that you can entrust my teachings to who can in turn teach others.

Again we see a mistranslation in the King James version which translates it as *"² And the things that thou hast heard of me among many witnesses, the same commit thou to faithful men, who shall be able to teach others also."*

Paul – the champion of women

There are other passages, too, from Paul's writings which have been misconstrued throughout church history and used to form a particular narrative that served certain agendas. As I said earlier, this is not an all-encompassing, comprehensive look at every verse that Paul wrote; but hopefully what I've shared here will show you that Paul was not against women taking public leadership roles in the New Testament churches. Paul, sadly, has been greatly misrepresented over the centuries. After Jesus, he was probably the most outspoken, and greatest, champion of women in the New Testament church; his words set in place a record, for all time, of the equality and worth of women in the church and in society.

Go Deeper

- Paul's statements about women seem to have overshadowed Jesus's views and treatment of women. Why do you think that is?

- Was Paul against women in leadership, as teachers etc? Has the information in this chapter changed how you see Paul?

- Think through the implications of Eph 5:21, "submitting yourselves one to another in the fear of the Lord". If mutual submission to one another on an equal basis is what Paul was actually meaning, what would that look like in our modern churches? How would that understanding change things?

- Think through the implications of the traditional understanding of "man as the head of the home" or "man as the spiritual head of the home" in light of what this chapter presents. How does the understanding of man and woman being given mutual leadership and commission to head up a family, change things? How would it change things in your marriage? …in our churches?

- If what is contained in this chapter is true, then what do we need to do to change things - as individuals, leaders, and as congregations? What needs to happen in our churches and families as a result?

- Women were excluded from leadership in the church over time – think about (and discuss) how this discrimination affected the church over the centuries.

If using this as a group study set next week's assignment – to read chapter 8, 'From Jesus and Paul to Today' – and think through the questions at the end of the chapter. Remember also to pray for the group or any individuals that need to be ministered to before finishing for the night.

References

1. https://www.myjewishlearning.com/article/three-blessings/

2. 1 Cor 1:13; 1 Cor 6:2,9,16,19; 1 Cor 7:16; 1 Cor 9:6,7,8,10; 1 Cor 10:22; 1 Cor 11:22; 1 Cor 14:36a,36b. Why Not Women – David Hamilton and Lauren Cunningham, YWAM Publishing Seattle 2000. Chapter 14 pages 190,191. Reference notes on Pg269 http://www.perseus.tufts.edu/hopper/text?doc=Perseus%3Atext%3A1999.04.0057%3Aalphabetic+letter%3D*h%3Aentry+group%3D1%3Aentry%3Dh%29%2F2

3. https://www.biblica.com/resources/scholar-notes/niv-study-bible/intro-to-1-timothy/

4. The Mirror Translation - Francois Du Toit, http://www.mirrorword.net
5. The Apostolic Woman by Linda Heidler with Chuck Pierce, GZI Publishing 2018, Pg 157

8
From Jesus and Paul to Today

A couple of centuries after Jesus ascended, having committed the emerging church into the hands of His disciples and followers, some fundamental changes began to occur. These changes took the church further and further away from the original example and teachings that Jesus left us with. Jesus and Paul clearly taught that women were men's equals and could follow the call of God on their life, including becoming leaders in the church. Even though Jesus and Paul taught and modelled that, the church went away from their example and teaching and joined society again in holding to the traditional view of woman as a lesser, subservient creature.

By the end of the second century the church had started to become institutionalised and even used for political purposes. Soon after that it split, because of differing opinions, into two divisions – the Eastern or Orthodox Church, and what would eventually become the Western Church as we know it today, which includes Catholicism and all our other western church denominations.

As Christianity spread, it did so in societies that functioned largely from a male supremacy model, and women leaders were seen to be a threat to that. Certain men began to deliberately teach and promote the idea that Paul was against women, changing his teachings to reflect that, and they downplayed the views and interaction of Jesus with women to reflect their ideas and agendas. During these early years women were slowly excluded from leadership positions, with many people's views in regards to women reverting back to those of the secular world around them. Once more women were seen as being less than men.

Tertullian, the second-century Latin church father, wrote in "On the Veiling of Virgins" *"It is not permitted to a woman to speak in church. Neither may she teach, baptize, offer, nor claim for herself any function proper to a man, least of all the sacerdotal office."* Yet there were still those who tried to defend women and stand up for their right to be all that Christ called them to be.

The church began to become institutionalised and by the beginning of the 3rd century it had become a place of political and cultural power struggles, where men vied for leadership positions and often did whatever was necessary to achieve the positions they wanted. This happened largely because in the early 3rd century the church was tied to political and cultural leadership by Emperors and Kings, such as Constantine and Tiridates the third, of Armenia, both of whom made Christianity the official religion of their kingdoms. In practice that meant that anyone wanting to hold a position of power in those kingdoms had to be a Christian. Of course that led to many saying that they were Christians, who weren't, just so they could keep, or gain, a job. Men also began to bribe and buy their way into positions of power within the church structure, filling the church with corruption, political intrigue, and schemes.

In the home women fared no better. In many nations women (and children) were considered to be the legal property of their husbands and fathers. That gave the men the right to do as they wished with their wives and children and, in many cases, be immune from prosecution. In many countries married women could not own properties of their own, or receive inheritances; these went automatically to their husbands. They also could not legally earn money of their own, or vote. Their husbands had the legal right to beat them, rape them, and treat them however they saw fit.

Limits established in serving God

In these early centuries of the church we see the beginnings of religious orders being established – for both men and women. Monasteries and convents began to be established, and for many women this was the only way that they could follow the call of God on their life, and devote themselves to His service, however this usually applied only to single women. Married women, who were called by God to serve Him, were forced to find their expression in serving the Lord in caring for their families, widows, and the poor.

As more convents arose the women leaders of those became women of influence and power, yet in the end, as great as that power was, it was still subservient to the men who ruled over them as Bishops, Popes etc. In the Roman Catholic and Eastern Orthodox Church, the priesthood and the ministries dependent upon it – such as Bishop, Patriarch and Pope – were restricted to men. At the first Council of Orange (441) they forbade the ordination of women as deacons. From that time on women were locked out of all leadership positions in the Church, except that of Abbess or Mother Superior, and these women were only allowed leadership of the women in their convents.

By the time of the Protestant Reformation in the 1500's both the Protestant and Roman Catholic churches had established convents, but the Reformation led to the closing of Protestant convents, leaving only Roman Catholic convents as places where women could formally serve the Lord.

From the time of those changes until the twentieth century the majority of churches upheld the traditional position of male headship, and they restricted leadership and preaching roles within the Church to men. Around the late nineteenth century and into the beginning of the twentieth century there arose a few exceptions to that, such as the Salvation Army, the Quakers, and Aimee Semple-McPherson's Pentecostal movement.

However it wasn't until the latter half of the twentieth century that women in the church began to stand up for their God-given right to be accepted as the equals He created them to be, and to be allowed to follow the callings that He had for them. From then until now we've seen great progress, but we still have a long way to go until the church is once again seen as the place where all are equal in God's sight, and are allowed to follow His call on their lives.

Changed identities and gender re-assignment in Scripture

In the next part of this chapter I want to look at something that, sad to say, actually happened and didn't get corrected until the early twentieth century.

Gender name changes, in literary circles specifically, are not a new thing. Over the years many women took a male nom-de-plume to protect their identity, or to enable them to get a publisher to accept them. Also sometimes, in translating other languages, one can be forgiven for making translation mistakes if one doesn't understand the complexities of certain languages, especially when it comes to the accidental misreading or misspelling of a name. But what I want to address here goes beyond accidental misreading and misspelling to the deliberate changing of sex and identities that happened to several women mentioned in the most sacred of literature – the Bible – in order to achieve a specific agenda.

Some of the women leaders and apostles of the early church were given name changes from female to male in Scripture, and the church even changed some of their other personal details. This was done by certain men in order to suit the agenda of the politically run, male dominated, church that arose from the mid 2nd century AD onwards.

These men began to change records and assign male names to the names of some of the women apostles and leaders of the early church that are mentioned in the New Testament to reinforce the male leadership favoured by the church of the day. That would lead to many centuries of women being looked upon by the church in unscriptural ways that certainly did not follow the example or teachings of either Jesus, Paul, or the other early apostles. Scripture would get twisted, and even in some places rewritten, to present a certain view that was different from the original view of the authors. Once again women became regarded as being deceived, evil in intent, less than men, second class, not of equal value, and not as gifted. They had no right to equal opportunities in callings, gifting, and more.

These ideas continued to take hold of the church until women could hold no positions of authority and were only allowed to do work like feeding the poor, praying, becoming nuns, missionaries or looking after other women or children. This continued for centuries and indeed was the viewpoint of most of the church right up until the mid-late 1900's, and in some places in the world it is still the prevalent opinion today.

These name changes and gender reassignment by historical church leaders and commentators had a huge impact on the church for centuries, promoting the idea that all New Testament leaders in the church were male, and that male leadership of the church was God's idea. It's only been in the last century that the Bible has been corrected, and the altered names changed back to the original female names.

That was the church that was around when I became a Christian – a place where women (myself included) were told that they could not function in certain gifts because of their gender, and who, while they could be missionaries, could not legally be a pastor or, in some cases, even teach those that they led to Christ. Any teaching or training had to be handed over to a man as soon as possible. Thankfully over the past fifty years that has begun to change, and while there have always been women who went against the norm, and were brave enough to follow God's call, they were definitely the exception.

I want to share the stories of the five women found in Scripture who were assigned male name changes in our Bibles.

Euodia and Syntyche *(Phil 4:2-3)*

Euodia and Syntyche had their names changed and became Euodias and Syntyches. Paul mentions these two women leaders, Euodia and Syntyche in the fourth chapter of Philippians, where he makes an appeal to them to be of the same mind. *"I plead with Euodia and I plead with Syntyche to be of the same mind in the Lord. Yes, and I ask you, my true companion, help these women since they have contended at my side in the cause of the gospel, along with Clement and the rest of my co-workers, whose names are in the book of life."* **(Phil 4: 2–3).**

Paul's letter to the Philippians differs to his other letters in that he specifically includes the supervisors / overseers (*episkopoi*) and ministers / deacons (*diakonoi*) in his opening greeting. Instead of the more usual English translation of "overseers and deacons", FF Bruce (1981) translates this phrase in Phil 1:1 as "chief pastors and other ministers", which more helpfully conveys the meaning of these ministry roles to modern readers. It is believed that Euodia, Syntyche, and Clement, who is mentioned with them, were the supervisors, or chief pastors, of house churches at Philippi. We know that Euodia and Syntyche are women because not only does it say so in these verses in the original manuscripts, but these were commonly used women's names in those times. Paul also used feminine plural pronouns, when talking about them, not male ones. Neither the male name "Euodias" nor "Syntyches" has been found in historical records, whereas "Euodia" and "Syntyche", as names of women, are common in inscriptions . . . [1]

Many commentators say that the whole of Philippians, with its emphasis on spiritual maturity, humility and unity, builds intentionally toward Paul's plea for these two women to be of the same mind. If they were simply congregation members Paul would more likely have addressed their elders telling them to settle the dispute between the two women. Even in asking a certain "true companion" to help, (using male pronouns) he gives a plea for this man to help them, not to exercise authority over them.

Church leader and historian John Chrysostom in the fifth century confirms that they were women, when he said, *"It seems to me that these women were the head of the church which was at Philippi."* [2] but many others disagreed.

Both Euodia and Syntche had their genders changed repeatedly throughout time and in various versions of Scripture. In the early King James Version Euodia appeared as the name of a man—"Euodias." Theodore of Mopsuestia (circa 350 – 428) tells of some who took Syntyche to be a man's name—Syntyches. He also mentions the fact that some held that Syntyches was the husband of Euodia, and that he was none other than the jailer who figures in the story of Acts 16.[3] [The Tyndale and Cranmer Scripture versions [William Tyndale and Thomas Cranmer] also make the second a man's name.

While Paul's reference to Euodia and Syntyche is short it does show the value that he places on them and their ministry, and it shows that he knew them and had worked directly with them in spreading the gospel throughout the city of Phillipi. He refers to them using the same terms as he used to describe Timothy and Epaphroditus and their work with him in spreading the gospel. (Phil 2:2, 25) [3] So, according to Paul, the ministries of the women Euodia and Syntyche were in some ways comparable to the ministries of the men Timothy and Epaphroditus.

Nympha *(Col 4:15)*

Nympha was changed to Nymphas and Scripture was amended to say, "…the church meets in *his* house."

In his epistle to the Colossians Paul specifically greets Nympha, acknowledging that she is a leader of the church, and that the church meets in *her* house. Those who had churches meeting in their homes assumed a pastoral role of some kind, and Nympha is one of several women in the New Testament who is given this position and assignment.

This reference to a female house church leader seems to have made some scribes uncomfortable. A number of early manuscripts were changed to reflect that, and "Nympha" was changed to "Nymphas" (a male version of her name). The King James Version and other early English translations (Darby, Douay-Rheims, Geneva Bible, Young's, etc.) favoured Nymphas, and spoke of the church meeting in *his* house. When Nympha was thought to be male she was readily described as the leader of that house church. John Eadie (1884) described a masculine Nympha as "worthy of distinction" because the church met in *"his"* house.[4]

John Davenant (1832) lamented that Ambrosiaster, in his commentary on Colossians, had *"transformed this pious and renowned man into a woman"* and insisted that it must be the error of *"some ignorant and lazy Monk"* who inserted the feminine into Ambrosiaster's text. He went on to describe Nympha as a *"distinguished man"* and postulated that *"the congregation of the faithful was accustomed to assemble in [Nympha's] house . . . because he instructed all his domestics piously and in a Christian-like manner, and trained them daily in religious exercises."*[5]

Thankfully, modern-day translators of Scripture have corrected this and Nympha again appears in her true identity as a woman in most modern Bible versions.

Junia *(Rom 16:7)*

Junia was changed to Junias. Paul calls this woman an 'apostle' in Romans 16:7. *"Greet Andronicus and Junia, my fellow Jews who have been in prison with me. They are outstanding among the apostles, and they were in Christ before I was."*

Notice, too, that Paul calls her "outstanding among the apostles". Junia was a first century apostle of note, as were the Twelve, Paul, and others mentioned in Scripture. The fact that she was a woman was not an issue to the early apostles, or the early church in general, as they had learnt well from Jesus and Paul that all were equal in God's Kingdom.

We know that Junia is a woman because there are historical records showing it was a well-used women's name at the time, and that there are no records of men named "Junia" from the first century. Neither are there any examples of men with names that are similar; for example, men named "Junias" or "Junianus" being nicknamed "Junia".

All of the early church fathers who commented on the passage also said that Junia was a woman, including Origen and John Chrysostom.

The first reference to Junia being male instead of female is from the *Index Discipulorum*, a document written by Epiphanius (315 - 403), purporting to list the seventy disciples whom Christ commissioned (Luke 10:1). In this document he makes both Priscilla and Junia into men. His views on women were full of vitriol and often scathing. He stated at the time in his writing, *"The female sex is easily seduced, weak and without much understanding. The Devil seeks to vomit out disorder through women... We wish to apply masculine reasoning and destroy the folly of these women."*

Junia eventually came to be known almost exclusively as a man, even though the weight of ancient evidence overwhelmingly favoured her being a woman. The King James version (and several others) referred to her in male form as "Junias". Even the ESV translation still footnotes "Junias" as an option. However, more and more, Junia's identity *as a woman* is being reinstated in Scripture, and her true identity restored.

Priscilla *(Acts 18:2, 18, 19, 26; Rom 16:3; 1 Cor. 16:19; 2 Tim. 4:19)*

Priscilla was renamed Prisca in the Bible and some men claimed she was not a female but a male, despite Paul specifically stating that she was a 'woman' (Acts 18:2). She was mentioned by name in the New Testament more times than some of the Twelve, yet those things didn't make her safe from having her gender reassigned. Epiphanius' Index Discipulorum also makes Priscilla into a man, and even makes her the bishop of a church nowhere near her husband's church.

The discomfort with Priscilla being a woman is most likely linked with both ancient convention and her eminence in teaching and church planting. Ancient societal convention dictated that a man's name usually came before his wife's, but Priscilla is mentioned before her husband Aquila five out of seven times, suggesting that she was the more prominent of the missionary couple. She instructed Apollos in the gospel (Acts 18:26), was a house church leader in Corinth, and some church historians and commenters have speculated that she may have written the Epistle to the Hebrews. No wonder she was seen as a threat.

In order for Prisca and Aquila to both be men they were said by church leaders to be men who ministered together, not husband and wife.

Church history sadly went far astray from Jesus's example and Paul's teachings, and their obvious respect for women as people and as leaders, but we are making a comeback now.

In the centuries that followed Jesus and Paul, the church regressed, re-embracing society's ungodly view of women, and joined them once again in holding women in a place of both derision, bondage and servitude.

Samuel Johnson, was regarded as one of the greatest literary figures of the 18th century and was a man who was honoured by his government and much of society for his contribution to literature. In James Boswell's book, "The Life of Samuel Johnson. LL.D." Boswell records a comment made by Samuel Johnson about women preachers in the Quaker church, *"A woman preaching is like a dog walking on it's hind legs, it's not done well; but you are surprised to find it done at all."*[18]

That statement by Samuel Johnson is typical of the prevailing attitude and prejudice of men against women throughout the centuries and sadly this sort of attitude is still prevalent in many places, even today.

How do we respond to this?

What should be our response to this knowledge? When I first found out about the deliberate repression, and even exclusion, of these women in church history, I was angry! I felt betrayed, hurt, and for a time felt wounded by the injustice that had been done, not only to them, but to all women throughout church history. I had to process through those feelings with the Lord in order to be able to share, not from a heart of bitterness and wanting to strike back, but from a heart of understanding culture and history, and of searching my heart to see where I had biases. I also had to ask the Lord what my part was in righting this wrong that had been done. I had to be able to share what I knew with a right motive and a clean heart. That process took a while, as I wrestled with the implications of this knowledge for my own life and the lives of the women I knew.

Some of you may be angry on reading this information – that is understandable. You have just had your faith in the leadership of the early church, and maybe even of Scripture, shaken. That will take some time and some processing to work through. Check out the information for yourself. Do your own research and study; don't just take my word for it. The information is out there and is not hard to find. Please, process it through with the Lord. Forgive those that have wronged you personally, or have wronged women throughout history, and even those who still do so today in the church. Process through the hurt and don't allow a root of bitterness to be established in your life (Heb 12:15).

Ask the Lord to help you treat all people as God Himself treats them – with love, honour and dignity, knowing that they are made in His image, as you are. Root out any biases in your heart towards other people, races, genders etc.

Paul rightly says in Gal 3:26-29, *"For you are all sons (children) of God through faith in Christ Jesus. For as many of you as were baptized into Christ have put on Christ. There is neither Jew nor Greek, there is neither slave nor free, there is no male and female; for you are all one in Christ Jesus. And if you are Christ's, then you are Abraham's seed, and heirs according to the promise."*

For the church to move forward and become all that God has in mind for it, we must be able to do so with honour in our hearts toward all people, without putting each other down, and realise that we all are called by God to play a part in His heart's desire – that all mankind would be reconciled and restored back to relationship with Him (2 Cor 5:18-21; Col 1:20-22) and that they may walk in freedom, enjoying life in all its fullness (John 10:10).

Go Deeper

- The early church started out well but, as we've seen, some people's agendas influenced the future of the church as it became more established from the 3rd century on. It became a place of political and cultural power struggles. What ongoing affect did that have on the church?

- What happened on a spiritual, emotional, mental and practical level for women as a result of discrimination?

- In reading the information about women's names being changed to men's in the Bible, how did that make you feel? What effect would that have had on the church? What do you think God felt about it happening?

- Looking at the church a century ago and where we are today – what has changed for women? Is the change enough or should there be more?

- Do we need to repent – on an individual level or church wide level for what has happened and how we've treated them? What restoration needs to be made if any?

- What can we do on an individual level, and a church wide level to encourage women to be all God has called them to be?

If using this as a group study set next week's assignment – to read chapter 9, 'Where we are today' – and think through the questions at the end of the chapter. Remember also to pray for the group or any individuals that need to be ministered to before finishing for the night.

● ● ● ● ● ● ● ●

References

1. Mopsuestia's commentary on Philippians names both these people correctly as women (see *Theodore of Mopsuestia: Commentary on the Minor Pauline Epistles*, trans. by Rowan A. Greer [Atlanta, Ga.: Society of Biblical Literature, 2010], 351), but it seems he related a differing opinion at another time.

2. J. Hugh Michael, *The Epistle of Paul to the Philippians* (Seattle, Wa.: Digital Publishing, 2018; originally published by Harper and Brothers in 1928), eBook Location 4186.

3. *Homilies on Philippians 13.*

4. John Eadie, *A Commentary on the Greek Text of the Epistle of Paul to the Colossians* (Edinburgh: T. T. Clark, 1884), 290.

5. John Davenant, *An Exposition of the Epistle of St. Paul to the Colossians*, Vol. 2 (London: Hamilton & Adams, 1832), 298-299. For more on Nympha, see Marg Mowczko's article, "Nympha: A House Church Leader in the Lycus Valley (Colossians 4:15)." https://margmowczko.com/nympha-house-church-colossians-415/

6. *Stromata* 3.6.53.

7. https://biblehub.com/commentaries/philippians/4-3.htm

8. https://www.britannica.com/biography/Samuel-Johnson/The-Lives-of-the-Poets

9. https://www.enotes.com/topics/life-samuel-johnson-ll-d/quotes/womans-preaching-like-dogs-walking-his-hind-legs

9
Where We Are Today

We live in an age where women can do any job in the world – almost!

One of the places women still struggle to find equality is within the church. Rena Pederson, Pulitzer Prize finalist and author of "The Lost Apostle" said this, *"A girl can grow up to be almost anything today – the commander of a NASA space station like Eileen Collins, or Secretary of State like Condoleeza Rice, or a Fortune 500 CEO like Anne Mulcahy of Xerox – but not a minister, or even a teacher, in some of the larger Christian denominations."*

Sadly in many parts of the church globally we still face widespread restrictions on what women can and can't do. Many still don't believe that God made women equal in worth and calling, or that God would call women to leadership roles in the church today. Sometimes they will agree that God made women equal in value, yet will still deny that He made them equal in calling.

Over the years, as I have endeavoured to share with people what Scripture says on this subject, many people have not understood that these were not my own ideas, or my childhood hurt reacting; I was actually teaching what Scripture teaches. As you'll read later, when I share my journey as a woman in ministry today, I have been called names and openly derided for daring to speak up about this subject. But if we do not declare truth and challenge false ideas and theology then things will not change. God is calling women everywhere to step up into their high calling as those made in His image, called like the original woman Eve, to multiply themselves in every way, and work side by side with men to establish God's Kingdom on earth.

If we are going to offer to people true freedom in Christ then some things need to change. We need to come back to a correct scriptural view of women and see them as God sees them. We need to give them the same rights and freedoms as men, not because we're following the world, or because of some women's liberation movement, or anything like that, but because it's what Scripture teaches and it's what Christ taught and modelled. We need our women to take their rightful God given place in church and society. The church should be leading the way in this area, encouraging women to be all that God calls them to be.

Come to Christ and be free

There is a world full of people who need to see women take their rightful place in the church, to see true freedom in action. We've said to women worldwide over the years, "Come to Christ and you'll be free" and then once they became Christians we've told them that because they're a woman they're restricted to being under submission to men and that they can only do certain things.

What sort of freedom is that? Is that really what Christ meant in John 10:10 when He said that He had come to give us life in all its fullness, or is the thief still being allowed to do his work of stealing from us all by putting women down, killing their hopes and dreams, and keeping women in one form of bondage or another? Is the place that we have offered women in the past really what the Trinity meant when they said, through Paul in Gal 3:28, "*There is neither Jew nor Gentile, neither slave nor free, there is no male and female, for you are all one in Christ Jesus. No one can claim a spiritual superiority.*" (AMP) The American Standard version says we are all "*one man in Christ Jesus*". That word man is a reference back to Eden where originally man and woman were known by the one name 'Adam', which means 'mankind'.

It's time for the church to truly offer freedom to everyone, and for all people, women included, to truly know that in Christ there is no condemnation, no shame, and that life in Christ really is an abundant, free life.

We need women to lead too!

True freedom to follow the call of God must apply to women as well as men.

It's time to see women apostles, prophets, teachers, evangelists, workers of miracles, missionaries, mothers, friends, CEO's, administrators, factory-workers, etc. be all that they are called to be – free to operate their gifts both inside and outside the church, free to follow the callings of God on their lives and release the Kingdom of God on earth with love and power.

Scripture and history tell us the stories of many women who followed the call of God on their lives over the centuries, such as Deborah, Phoebe, Lydia, Teresa of Avilla, Joan of Arc, Mother Theresa, Maria Woodworth-Etter, Aimee Semple McPherson, Kathryn Kuhlman, and others. These women stepped up, defied convention and followed the call of God on their lives, however they were often the odd one out, the ones who defied society's norm. But their pioneering lives opened the door for all women to step back into the original plan that God had for them.

Over the last century or so we've seen a restoration of the gifts of the Spirit to the church and a restoration of what is often called 'five-fold' gifts – evangelists, pastors, teachers, prophets and apostles – those whose calling is, amongst other things, to help bring the church to maturity, and to train and equip those in the church for their works of ministry. *"And he gave the apostles, prophets, evangelists, pastor's, and teachers, [12]to equip the saints for the work of ministry, for building up the body of Christ, [13]until we all attain to the unity of the faith and of the knowledge of the Son of God, to mature manhood, to the measure of the stature of the fullness of Christ..."* Eph 4:11-13.

These apostles, prophets, teachers, pastors and evangelists will have both men and women in their ranks. They will be called and equipped by God to work together, and that will increase in the days ahead.

Recently the Lord gave me a prophetic word about the emergence of women apostles in this time. If you'd like to read that word it can be found here - https://www.nzpropheticnetwork.com/the-emerging-women-apostles-by-lyn-packer

The church is built on the foundation of apostles and prophets – sent ones and proclaimers of God's heart. In Eph 2:19-22 it tells us, *"So then you are no longer strangers and aliens, but you are fellow citizens with the saints, and are of God's household, [20]having been built on the foundation of the apostles and prophets, Christ Jesus Himself being the corner stone, [21]in whom the whole building, being fitted together, is growing into a holy temple in the Lord, [22]in whom you also are being built together into a dwelling of God in the Spirit."*

The church was built on the revelation given to the apostles and prophets – Christ in all, and filling all, with Him being the corner stone, the stone from which all other living stones take their alignment and find their place. Many of the early church's apostles and prophets were women and they were held in the same high regard as male apostles and prophets were.

Throughout the church worldwide over the last century in particular we've seen women taking their very necessary place as ministers of God's love and grace in the church and in society. I am one of these women and my journey has been fairly typical of many women as we've struggled to find our value, identity and place in the church.

My personal journey

This book is in reality the story of my journey, discovering my heritage and my inheritance as a woman created in God's image. I've been a Christian now for many years, since my mid-teens, having been saved and called by God into ministry at the age of sixteen. From my early twenties I've been in some form of leadership role in youth groups, Christian ministries or churches as a senior co-pastor with my husband and as a prophet. I'm now in my mid 60's, so that's over 40 years of ministry. During that time I've seen how women, including myself have been treated in the church, and I've been on the receiving end of ministry bias and even verbal abuse for my views on a woman's place and role in the church. I've been called a feminist and a Jezebel, I've been told that I couldn't function in my gifts and calling, and have been denied opportunities because of my gender and much more.

If I am a feminist then it is in the true sense of the word, which means simply – *'relating to, or supporting, women'*. If I am a feminist then I am a Jesus type of feminist because I believe, support, and live out the views that Jesus, Holy Spirit and the Father have of women. I have strong views and beliefs, and I am unafraid to voice them and substantiate them, so if being strong makes me a Jezebel then every woman who has ever stood up for herself is probably also one. (I also think those people who called me that need to do some study themselves to find out who Jezebel was and what that spirit actually does). As far as my gifts and calling go, they came from God and I must be obedient and faithful in using them, as we all must.

The childhood days

The things that happen in your life as a child have a powerful impact on you, shaping your beliefs and worldview – in particular what you think about yourself, and your place in the world. They can also have a huge effect on shaping your Christian life.

Some of the things that had a huge effect on shaping my life came from being part of a family where sexual and physical abuse, along with emotional manipulation and control, were commonplace. I was one of nine children and of those nine, six of us that we know of were sexually abused by Dad or Grandad, and all of us were beaten and abused verbally, physically and emotionally. My Dad and Grandad both sexually abused me over a period of sixteen years. Physical beatings where my father lost control of himself meant that we lived under a lot of fear and intimidation. There were times when we would go to school with our clothes sticking to the welts on our backs and then get in trouble because we couldn't sit still (comfortably) in class because of those welts.

My mother was a white witch, clairvoyant, manipulator and abuser, constantly making us feel like we were never good enough, or were somehow to blame for everything that happened. Her words continually shut you out or cut you down. That, combined with Dad and Granddad's sexual and physical abuse, left me feeling that I was worth nothing and would never amount to anything. I suffered severe PTSD as a result of the years of abuse I suffered and this later manifested in bouts of depression and 25 years of fibromyalgia.

I lived in a world where the reality of life was too horrible to face, so my escape mechanisms meant that I suppressed as many memories as I could by retreating into a frozen dead-like state when the abuse happened. I lived in an internal fantasy world, and loved school, as it was an escape from home life.

I lived with my parents until I was twelve, when I was sent to live with my grandparents. That was like going from the frying pan into the fire itself. While my father had sexually abused me, my grandfather was a sadistic abuser who used fear and threats of death to rule over me and my grandmother. As a result I was put on Valium at thirteen years old and didn't come off it until I was twenty. How I came off Valium is a story of God's goodness in the midst of cold-turkey withdrawal, but that's a story for another day.

From my perspective being female was the worst thing in the world. A female had no rights, she was born to be under the control of the men in her life, who had the right to do to her what they chose, and the right to make the final decisions regarding her life – even down to such things as what jobs she could, or could not, do.

I don't tell you any of this to make you feel sorry for me, but to tell you my background so that you can understand what shaped my beliefs about myself and my place in the world, and how that later affected me as I started to live as a Christian and came into church life.

I knew very little of the church and its views on women, which is not surprising really, given my upbringing. But when I was sixteen, while living with my grandparents, the daughter of one of their friends invited me to a youth group meeting. I didn't want to go. I had a very low opinion of the church, but getting out of the house was better than sitting around watching the adults drink themselves into a violent state, so I went. To this day I am so glad I did, as that night changed the course of my life.

For the first time in my life I heard that I was loved, that God the Father, and Jesus, loved me so much that Jesus died so I could be loved and free. I was undone. The things I had longed for my whole life were being offered to me – love and freedom.

Entering the Church

As a young Christian I didn't realise at first that church life was yet another world where women were not free from control, even though I had been promised freedom in Christ. My brokenness and childhood beliefs had shaped my life in such a way that I didn't think to question what I was told by church leaders – that it was God's will and plan that women live in submission to men and be restricted in what they were allowed to do.

Within a few months of becoming a Christian I felt the Lord tell me very clearly that He was calling me to serve Him as a prophet and leader, to speak on His behalf and to train and teach His people, and I determined that I would follow that call, no matter what. Little did I know what that would mean, and the trouble it would get me into with the church, over the years.

As the years went by I became an assistant youth group leader in my church and in a nationwide Christian youth movement called Campus Life. Eventually, a few years later, through Campus Life, I met my husband Rob – a man who treated me with such respect and love that it confused me. I couldn't understand why he was so nice; I'd never had a man respect me as he did. He didn't try and take advantage of me or force me to do things I didn't want to do. It took me a while to see, and accept, that this was how a woman was supposed to be treated. But it would still be many years before I felt that I could trust him fully; I was always looking for him to prove that my childhood beliefs about men were true, yet he never did. I learnt so much about who God is, and how He loves, through how my husband loved and treated me. The love of my husband and the love of God brought much healing into my life.

God had so much healing to do in my life, but with His love, goodness and patience He has brought me to a place where I am no longer that same person. It took years of Him busting through walls I'd built up, through lies that I believed about myself, of showing me the truth, of healing ministry, and even deliverance. Over the years, however, the real, and free, me has emerged and stands today as a confident woman who knows that she has value, is loved, and who knows that she is destined to make a difference in the world she lives in.

God's call to ministry

Both my husband and I had strong calls of God on our lives and we determined to follow them. He eventually became a pastor, and while my husband was accepted as a pastor, we women could not be called that, or hold a pastoral position in our denomination at that time. I could be a pastor's wife, but not a pastor myself, and I certainly could not, according to the leaders in all the churches that I knew of, be a prophet. In our Pentecostal church I could prophesy as a woman, but not be a prophet, even though God had told me Himself that it was what He was calling me to be. I was told point blank by several pastors that the reason I could not be a prophet was because I was a woman. What they also said was that being a prophet would put me in a position of authority over men, and the Bible said that I had to be in submission to them.

According to them my gender meant that I could not follow what I believed was the call of God on my life. So, to them, that also meant that because I believed that God had called me to be a prophet I must be deceived about what I thought my calling was, and when I pushed against that I was told that I had a Jezebel spirit. I didn't have a Jezebel spirit, but my instinctive knowledge that this discrimination was wrong, and my desire for justice, coupled with my unresolved childhood hurts, meant that I pushed back unwisely and, at times, argumentatively, which in their minds confirmed their opinion that I was a deceived, out of order, rebellious woman with a Jezebel spirit.

Around this time, the mid 1980's, our denomination decided that pastors' wives could be acknowledged as pastors, but they still could not lead a church. However very few of us were officially recognised as such, or ordained into that role; that didn't come until later. Sadly often what happened is that the pastors' wives were given that title, but the underlying discrimination that had been going on for centuries was never addressed or apologised for, and no correct scriptural understanding was given to congregations.

In 1990 when I was in my mid-thirties the Lord started to deal with my childhood abuse in order to bring healing to me, and in that process an anger toward men in authority flared up within me that surprised me, although it probably shouldn't have, considering my childhood. This caused a huge dilemma for me. After all, I'd been taught by the church that women were to be submitted to men's leadership and that men in authority, such as church leaders, as well as their husbands, were in authority over them and were their covering. Yet here I was angry at men in authority and the control they seemed to have over my life, and I was also angry at God because I thought at the time that He had given them that authority!

Discovering the truth

I didn't want to displease God or be out of His authority order, but I desperately wanted to know what was right, what Scripture actually taught, so I set out to study Scripture, and church history, on this subject for myself, and I did so for several years. Over those years the Lord took me on an extraordinary twin journey – of personal healing and dismantling wrong mind-sets about myself and how I viewed the world, and also of discovering how He viewed women, and the glorious plan that He had for them when He created them.

During that time I looked at both church and secular history and how different societies viewed, and treated, women throughout history. I delved deeply into the original meanings of words in Scripture, and the historical and cultural context of those Scriptures. I studied and read commentaries, and church history books, and records from both early church fathers and modern writers.

Many of those references and commentaries supported traditional church views, whereas what I found in Scripture itself, as I delved into original meanings, contradicted much of traditional church teaching on women. I finally figured out that the contradictions were there because of this truth – unless God gives us revelation we will usually only see in Scripture what is in our current theological framework of understanding. I realised that the people who had written those commentaries and concordances had viewed Scripture through certain theological and cultural lenses, and those lenses had coloured their thinking and approach to certain Scriptures. That made me realise even more that I needed to be careful not to read into Scripture what I wanted it to say.

The more I studied the more I found centuries of misunderstanding of Scripture, and at certain times in history, deliberate misrepresentation and downright dishonesty by some, in what had been taught about a woman's role in church and society. I found centuries of historical suppression, despising, and abuse of women that stood in direct opposition to God's original design and plans for how man and woman should interact and work together.

As you can imagine, I now had some dilemmas to face. My study had led me to believe the opposite of what the church had taught me. I had come to believe that God created women equal in value to men, and gave them both the same commission, inheritance and destiny. And, as I saw all through Scripture, they were also given equal right to follow the call of God on their lives as individuals. I was now faced with the dilemma of what this would mean for me personally – in my relationship with my husband, with the church, in my calling from God, and added to that, I wondered if people would believe me, and how was I going to share what I'd discovered?

Walking out the truth

It wasn't an easy thing being brave enough to share what I discovered with my husband Rob. He had grown up in a Christian home and had always only known, and been taught, the traditional church view on women. In the church he attended women were even required to wear head coverings in church services. While different denominations had different cultural applications of Scripture in regards to women, at that time they all believed the traditionally held view of a woman's place in the home and in the church being that of being submitted or subservient to male headship. In our marriage Rob believed that he was the head of the home and the priest of the family, with the governance of the family being on his shoulders, according to God's order; and while I could offer opinions and we could discuss things, in the end he believed that he had the final decision over any important matters and our marriage reflected that, with me always giving way to him in everything.

I eventually got up the courage to ask him to look at my research and he agreed to do so. I still remember the day he came out of his office weeks later, looked at me and said, "I've been taught wrong all my life."

Now here we were with our beliefs turned inside out, demolished, and being rebuilt by God, believing something radically different from what either of our backgrounds had taught us. That set us on a journey of figuring out what true equality looked like in a marriage, and how team leadership and responsibility for a family worked. It meant learning how to hear each other's hearts on a deeper level and to trust each other's intent. It also meant relearning how to process decisions together until we reached agreement, instead of me deferring to him for the sake of peace and being in submission. It meant realising that the call on my life was as important as the call on Rob's, and us learning together how to follow those calls as a couple and as individuals.

As pastors of a church and part of a leadership team we also had to navigate the fact that we now had different understandings of Scripture from those we worked alongside and those we pastored. We had to learn to model and share our new beliefs with humility, patience and strength of conviction, while giving people the space to process and question. The pressure to be quiet and not rock the boat was very real during those early days (and still is today actually). Many people – men and women – did not want to know what I had discovered. Many men did not want their position of authority to be disturbed, either as head of the home or as pastors. Many women didn't want to face the possibility that they had lived under a lie all their lives, and neither did the men. I was labelled a feminist and trouble maker by some, and a heretic by others. I was called deceived, Jezebel, and labelled as divisive. Yet, at the same time God was also revealing the truth of what Scripture said to others around the world, and I was suddenly not alone on this journey; God was starting to bring truth and reformation to the church in this area. It wasn't easy in those early days and it's still not easy today, a quarter of a century later. I've had many bad things said to me over the years – some by men, and some by other women who didn't understand what Scripture actually says about the place of women in God's plans.

My husband and I have been in church leadership for over forty years now, in many different roles – youth group leaders, worship pastors, assistant pastors, senior pastors and as a prophet. For the last twenty-something years our role has been that of itinerant ministers; this takes us into many churches in many nations. What I've found as we travel is that much of the church, both male and female, are, even today, trapped in paradigms that are unscriptural and which do not represent the true nature and character of the Trinity and their original plan for women.

Today I minister alongside my husband as well as heading up two seperate ministries that I started, Together Network (a ministry for supporting and empowering women in ministry leadership positions) and the New Zealand Prophetic Network (a ministry that broadcasts the prophetic words of New

Zealand prophets and supports and trains emerging and established prophets).

I believe that the church, and how it works, has so many good aspects to it, so the things I say here are not because I have something against the church; they are because I love it and willingly give my life for it. But unless we actually face the facts concerning how things are, we cannot change the things that need to change.

There are generations that will follow after us and unless we actually work through this they will be facing the same restricting beliefs and lies in their generations. Much change has already happened, but we still have a long way to go before we truly walk free. Let's not be the ones who cause our children and our children's children to have to deal with this all over again, Let's get it sorted out now so that we can get on with releasing heaven into earth, stewarding the earth wisely and preserving it intact for future generations, and seeing men and women everywhere being brought into freedom. This is our hope and our goal.

[20] For the creation was subjected to frustration, not by its own choice, but by the will of the one who subjected it, in hope [21] that the creation itself will be liberated from its bondage to decay and brought into the freedom and glory of the children of God." Rom 8:20,21.

The Trinity are bringing us back to fully being able to experience the freedom that they desired for us from the beginning, and we all get to play our part in seeing that happen. I'm excited about that and I hope you are too. I don't know about you, but I can't wait until all mankind experience the glorious freedom of being one of God's children.

Go Deeper

- Is discrimination still a big problem that affects women in the church today or have the changes over the last couple of decades been enough to halt discriminatory attitudes in today's church? …in your church? . . . in your marriage? . . . in your life?

- Ask the Lord what your part is in changing the beliefs and culture of your marriage, your church. Get very practical in thinking about this. The Lord has a part for you to play in changing things, whether through praying, teaching, or modelling freedom etc.

- Are there people you need to apologise to? Are there things you need to repent of? (understanding that 'repent' doesn't mean feeling bad, it means changing your mindset and coming into agreement with God's mind on a matter, and living accordingly.)

- Does this subject need to be well taught in our churches? If so, what are some ways that can happen?

- My story of discriminatory attitudes, statements and behaviours towards me is just one of thousands upon thousands down through the years, as women have dared to follow the call of God on their lives despite the beliefs of the church in general. Many have been wounded, and have even left church to go into secular business, because the discrimination was so severe. What can be done to bring healing to these women?

- You may have been wounded yourself, as a woman or man who wanted to follow God's call, and felt like you were discriminated against or not understood etc. Ask the Lord to show you any lies that the enemy has caused you to believe about yourself, your church, the other sex, your pastor, society. Let Him expose the lies and bring truth and healing, so that you can live free. This may be hard, but it will be worth it. Believe me, I know from experience.

If using this as a group study set next week's assignment – to read chapter 10, 'Into the Future' – and think through the questions at the end of the chapter. Remember also to pray for the group or any individuals that need to be ministered to before finishing for the night.

10
Into the Future

It's time for Paul's admonition of *"neither Jew nor gentile, male nor female, slave nor free"* to be truly established in the church!

Over the years people in church leadership have said to me that they believe women are equal to men in value before God, but at the same time that they are subservient to men as people, in the home, in leadership, or in calling. Other church leaders have said that they believe that women can be called by God to any gift and function in the church, but what is outworked in their churches shows that this is still not yet truly the case. I know that pastors and church leaders are tasked with the job of bringing their congregation on that journey of understanding, and that it is not easy, but all too often, while their personal beliefs may have changed, there is still very little being done in the way of teaching congregations what Scripture actually says, or of modelling the truth.

I see many male pastors and leaders whose wives are now called pastors, but they still believe that their wives should be under their authority in the home. Many of those same male pastors also still don't seem to recognise the leadership gifts and callings on other women in their churches, or if they do, they still relegate women to leadership roles in things like Sunday school leader, mission work, or prayer ministry. Too few churches are actively training the women that sit in their congregations to fulfil the call of God on their lives, whether that call is as apostles, prophets, teachers, CEO's, business women, etc.

In church after church we still see pulpit time being given to men while women, who may have an equal calling as teachers and an equal depth of understanding of Scripture, have to sit quietly, knowing that their calling is being unrecognised, or worse, sometimes even ignored by their pastors for varying reasons.

Where training in relation to gifting and calling from God is happening in churches, there can still often be either unconscious, or sometimes conscious, discrimination happening. For example a woman I know was part of a church where the pastor said several times over a period of years that he recognised her calling and function as a prophet with a national and international ministry, and that he wanted her to do some teaching on prophecy for the church, and to preach in the main Sunday service, but it never happened. At the same time a male prophet in the same church who had less experience and a far smaller ministry influence, was regularly given opportunity to share and teach from the pulpit. What does this say, and what are women to think, when something like this happens? As a woman the temptation is there to process that as discrimination, even though that may not have been the pastor's heart at all.

I also know of a pastor who is currently running a training group for the men in his church that have the same call on their life as he has on his – to be an apostle – but he can't see that he is possibly discriminating against the women in the church who have that calling by limiting the group to male only. I know that he has some reasons that make sense to him as to why he has limited the group to men only, but it sends a powerful unspoken message to every woman in the church who has the calling to be an apostle – your call is not as important to me, the church, or to God, as a man's call.

Recently I was talking to a woman whose church is starting to go through the process of changing their policies on women in leadership and the male Senior Pastor sees no point in apologising to the women in the congregation for past attitudes, or in providing the church with scriptural understanding for the changes they are making. He commented that he just wants to make the changes to their constitution and move on.

These are just a few of the discrepancies that we still face, and need to work through, and it's vital that we do so. If we are to truly offer freedom from bondage when we present the gospel to people then we must address the issue of how women are viewed and treated in the church.

It's time for the church to truly offer freedom to everyone, and for the world to know that life in Christ really is an abundant, free life with no condemnation, shame or inequality for either male or female.

It's time to see women free to operate their gifts, both inside and outside the church, free to follow the calling of God on their lives and to release the Kingdom of God on earth with love and power. There are women apostles, prophets, teachers, evangelists, pastors, workers of miracles, missionaries, mothers, friends, CEO's, administrators, factory-workers, etc. patiently waiting to be able to follow their callings with freedom, and to stand alongside men as true equals in bringing heaven to earth.

God has missed out also

Not only have men and women missed out because of what happened – the Trinity and the Kingdom of Heaven have missed out on so much, too. They've missed out on seeing the mandate that they gave, both in the beginning and through Christ, fulfilled as they had hoped up until now, but we are being given a chance to be a part of that happening. We can give Christ what He died and rose again for. We can fulfil the great commission if we work together, releasing the love of the Trinity into every sphere of society, every culture, and every nation.

When we come back to God's original blueprint for how men and women were created to function together, the church will be free to grow and mature as it should, every part of the Body working together in unity and harmony (see 1 Cor 12). Just think how much easier that will make it to get on with what we've actually been commissioned to do!

Our part in God's glorious plan

Each of us has a part to play in this story – the story of the fullness of redemption, of all people everywhere (including women) being liberated and set free to be all that God called them to be.

Why is it so important that the church deal with this? Because women everywhere need to be free, not just women in the church. I recently read this statement by a woman who provides fair pay employment for women (in a country where it is hard to find work that pays a decent wage to women). The woman mentioned in this statement is one of her workers. It shows some of the restrictions that women all around the world still face.

"She's not allowed to be out of the house at meal times. She has to be there to serve the men their food and wait on them while they eat. After they've eaten, then the women in the house can sit and eat. So, we negotiated her leave from the house at a time that wouldn't inconvenience the men. I took her to a nearby cafe to celebrate her birthday, which they don't do at home. Gifts and brunch on me. We sent selfie photos to her husband, as we were instructed to do so by him, (to prove we were where we said we would be). Despite her serious photo face (smiling and laughing can lead to accusations of being flirtatious), a fun time was had. She felt special. She tasted freedom."

How incredibly sad, that this woman and thousands like her around the world still do not have basic rights and freedoms.

What is your part in God's plan of redemption and freedom? Maybe it's you living free yourself, being an example to all who know you of what true freedom looks like. Maybe you're called to help other people find freedom, to bring healing, or to teach and disciple people into freedom and wholeness.

Women

If you're a woman you may have experienced some of the prejudices I've talked about. Maybe you've believed in your heart that God made you equal in worth and calling, but you've had no scriptural foundation for that. Can I encourage you to do some study so that you can share what Scripture really says in regards to this.

Or maybe, like I did, you've been hurt by people who have actively tried to dissuade you from following God's call on your life, simply because you're a woman. If that's the case please deal with that hurt to stop it becoming bitterness. Allow God to heal any wounds – let Him unveil the often hidden things such as anger, grief, rejection, childhood woundedness, etc. that all feed into that hurt. Forgive the men (and women) that you need to forgive, and ask the Lord to give you the grace to work alongside them in a way that honours both you and them, and the call of God on your lives.

Also deal with any bitterness in your heart that may be there toward God for what you've been through. I didn't realise how much offense I had held in my heart toward the Trinity for what I believed were their views on women, and for allowing the church to do these things to women. Ask them to give you revelation of how they see you, how loved you are by them, and the dreams that they have in their heart for you; it will bring much healing to you.

If you don't know what the call of God is on your life ask Him what He has for you to do, what gifts He has given you, and step out and use them. Make the difference you were created to make, and do it unashamedly – with both boldness and wisdom.

Women, who does God see when He looks at you?

I want to share with you this encouragement –

- When people looked at Eve and saw a deceived seducer, and the cause of the fall of mankind, God saw a woman He loved and had forgiven, who was made in His image, was full of glory and the mother of all mankind.

- When people looked at Sarah and saw a barren woman, God saw the mother of many nations.

- When people looked at Rahab and saw a prostitute, God saw someone worthy of being part of the lineage of Jesus.

- When people looked at Mary Magdalene and saw a demon-possessed woman, God saw the apostle to the apostles.

- When people looked at Joan of Arc and saw a teenager who heard voices and was believed to be a witch, God saw someone who would love and revere Him, following His call on her life gladly even if following Him meant death.

- When people looked at Maria Woodworth-Etter and saw a divorced and re-married woman trying to be a preacher, God saw a powerful, miracle working woman full of faith and trust.

- When Heidi Baker saw in herself a failed missionary with little fruit to show for years of serving God, God saw an apostle to the nations who would inspire and call people back to intimate relationship with Him, and who would become the mother to thousands of orphans.

When you look at your own life what do you see? Be encouraged – who you were yesterday, and even who you are today, is not the end of your story; God sees something different, something far different. There is greater glory for you to walk in yet, and a greater effect for your life to have in the earth!

Men – dealing with the perceived threats to manhood

The world has lost out on so much because of what happened. Men have lost so much, yet for many men, the thought of women walking in freedom is a threat – to their place, their manhood, their authority; but is that the truth? Is women's freedom really a threat to men, or is that another lie that they've believed?

Women's freedom can only be perceived as a threat if men want to hold fast to their false place of position, superiority, ego and pride, and to the lies that they've believed about women. If men long for true freedom then they must realise that seeing women walk in all that God created them to walk in will also set them free. Only then will they be free to no longer have to expend energy and time in defending a lie that needs to die. Men will be free to live without the fear that a woman may try to exert a false place of authority over them, or steal the gifts and positions that they perceive as belonging to them.

Letting go

Men, will it be easy to let go of the lies that you've believed, and the ego and pride that you've let drive you? Probably not. It may take facing the truth and realising that much of what you've believed has been wrong, wrestling with your beliefs, an honest searching of the heart, repenting and coming out of agreement with the lies, and into agreement with God. It means that you will need to admit that you have wounds, and allow the Lord to heal them. It may mean that your slave-driver fears, or even the outside forces that drive you, may need breaking off your life. It will probably mean that you have to apologise, ask forgiveness, and make restitution to some of the women you know. You will also have to be prepared to rebuild trust by proving consistently over time that any changes you make are a genuine, long-term change of heart, mind, attitude, and actions.

Pastors

If you're a pastor reading this book can I ask you to do your own research on this subject. Then look at how you and your eldership have viewed and treated women. Assess it honestly in light of what has been revealed to you in this book and in your own research.

Repent of any biases that the Holy Spirit reveals to you and consider whether you need to make personal, or public, apologies to the women in your congregation for the way that they have been treated, overlooked and shut down.

Consider doing some teaching on this subject with your congregation, and then follow that up with true equality – recognise and release the gifts on people's lives, regardless of their gender.

Pray for the women in your congregation – that their wounds would be healed. Pray that they would realise their value and know what their gifts and callings are; help them find out what they are, if possible, then make a place for them to function in their God given gifts and callings. Encourage and train women to find their spiritual gifts and callings, and follow the leading of Holy Spirit in them.

Let's build the future together

Let's finish by going back to the original plan of God in Genesis 1 and the mandate He gave to man and woman.

"[26]Then God said, "Let us make mankind in our image, in our likeness, so that they may rule over the fish in the sea and the birds in the sky, over the livestock and all the wild animals, and over all the creatures that move along the ground."[27]So God created mankind in his own image, in the image of God he created them; male and female he created them. [28]God

blessed them and said to them, "Be fruitful and increase in number; fill the earth and subdue it. Rule over the fish in the sea and the birds in the sky and over every living creature that moves on the ground." [29]Then God said, "I give you every seed-bearing plant on the face of the whole earth and every tree that has fruit with seed in it. They will be yours for food. [30]And to all the beasts of the earth and all the birds in the sky and all the creatures that move along the ground—everything that has the breath of life in it—I give every green plant for food." And it was so."

We were created in the image of God! Yet we now try and create our own image, and define others by the image we have of them. It's time for both of us, men and women, to surrender our ego, our fears, and our pride.

This is what we were created for, to fulfil God's mandate together, side by side. God's plan has never changed; He never recalled that mandate, or the complementary gifts that He gave us to help us fulfil it.

All along He had a plan to bring man and woman back to the original blueprint. He has done His part, now the future is in our hands. We can repeat what has gone before us in previous centuries or we can co-create a new future; the choice is ours, and now is the time that we need to make that choice.

Men, can I ask you, please have open hearts to hear the Spirit of God in this. Don't let the voice of tradition and the lies of the enemy speak louder in your heart and mind than the voice of God. What you do with the information in this book, and the prophetic call of God to us all that it contains, is critical. Ask God to reveal truth to you; search it out, check the information in this book to see if what I've shared is true. There is so much to gain, and also so much to lose!

There's not much point in us ladies getting free if we don't have you, side by side with us, as our equals in freedom. Our freedom will not be true freedom unless you, too, are fully free.

And then let's go change the world together!

Go Deeper

- Ask the Lord, "What do we need to do to ensure that future generations of women are truly free to be all that You call them to be?"

- What changes do I need to make in my attitudes and actions to portray what following Jesus in real freedom as a woman looks like?

- What changes do I need to make in my attitudes and actions to portray what following Jesus in real freedom as a man looks like?

- Why will my living free matter – in my family, in my church, in society?

- It has taken centuries to get where we are today, and it will take some time for change to happen. Ask the Lord, "What attitudes do I need to have toward my pastor and church as we embark on working through this? How can I support them, even when change may be slower than I'd like?"

How to Use This Book as a Study Guide

Individually or for group study

As you read this book you may find that you want to highlight passages or write notes in the margins of the pages. Feel free to do so, but be aware that if you do you probably won't want to lend the book to anyone else. I often find that I end up buying an extra copy of books I think I'll write in so that I have my copy and one I can loan out.

Use the book as a personal study guide

This book can be used as a basis for study, either individually or in your church. It provides a great opportunity to explore what Scripture says about God's glorious plan for His children – both male and female. The things it contains will cause you to ask serious questions and search for answers. I hope that they will cause you to search both Scripture and church history to see if the things contained in this book are true.

Curiosity and questions are both vitally important in discovering truth. They are the basis for all discovery and learning. Questions drive thinking and life forward. They invite conversation, understanding, knowledge, and growth and allow us to challenge our preconceived ideas and assumptions. We must therefore ask questions with an open mind, otherwise we will resort to looking and listening for information that validates our point of view, and ignore any evidence that contradicts it.

At the end of each chapter of this book you'll find questions that you can use individually or for group discussion. These questions will help you think through, and process, what the church has taught throughout the centuries, your current beliefs, and what you've read in that chapter. This will bring you into a greater understanding of how church culture has shaped your life, and will bring insight that I know the Spirit of God will use to take you to a new place of growth and understanding.

How to use this book as a study guide for groups

This book would be a great book for small group study for both women and men – either in a specially set up group or in a Home Group. To use this book as a group study you will need to set aside ten weeks. The following are some practical guidelines for facilitating such a group.

- Each individual will need their own copy of the book so they can read the appropriate chapter during the week and think through the questions at the end of each chapter before meeting together as a group.

- I suggest keeping your groups small – between 8 to 16 members is usually best. That's enough to still hold a discussion if several are absent, but not so many that discussions become unwieldy.

- May I recommend that meeting once a week, or every two weeks, is best. Anything more than that will not give people time to process what they've read on a personal level. If you meet less frequently than that you will often run the risk of them forgetting to do the reading and activations during the intervening time.

- Choose a group facilitator – someone who will oversee the discussion; you may already have this in place in a home group type setting. The facilitator's role is –

    - To create a safe space where people feel free to take an active part in the group.

    - To facilitate – not to take over the meeting or to take on the role of an expert. (If they do so it becomes more of a seminar and less of a group interacting with each other.)

    - To help the group adhere to commonly agreed group expectations.

- To facilitate discussion and to see that quieter people get included in the discussion and that more extroverted people don't monopolise it.

- To help the group stay on focus so the discussion doesn't wander off into unrelated topics.

• Set out any group expectations or guidelines for involvement, such as

- Bring your study guide (and Bible) with you each week to refer to as we go through the meeting.

- Honour each other by coming regularly and on time.

- Do any assignments for the session.

- Come prepared to share – your input is important.

- Understand any expectations for healthy discussion. Discuss and come to agreement as a group on what expectations you have concerning this.

- Agree to disagree respectfully. This means that the group members should agree to respect each other's opinions and not let opinions become arguments or personal.

- Encourage one another; be open to different opinions and to having your ideas challenged.

- Stay on focus.

• Have the group read one chapter a week, ahead of your meeting time, and do the individual activations at home. Then when you come together you can discuss how this went and encourage each other, using the questions provided at the end of each chapter to promote further discussion.

The questions are a starting place; you may get through all of them, or only one or two, in a meeting. The goal isn't to get through them all but to encourage open and honest discussion about what God has in His heart for both men and women, and their place in the church and society.

At the end of each discussion time take a few minutes to make sure that everyone is okay before you finish your time together. I encourage you to spend some time at the end of each session and pray with each other concerning the things that came up during the discussion.

Please feel free to contact me if you have questions, or to share testimonies of the things God has done in your life as a result of reading and studying the content of this book. The address for contacting me is on the author page at the end of the book.

Group study week 1 – Starting week

- Talk about the aims for the group; spend some time looking at the chapter on how to use the book individually, and as a group. As a group discuss and set any group expectations or guidelines for involvement. Write them out and make sure that everyone is in agreement with them; that way as you go forward you can hold each other accountable to the group agreement if you need to.

- Get each person to share what they hope to get out of the study, what expectations they have, and any reservations that they may have. Pair the people up and get them to pray for each other about the things they've just shared.

- Share about the possibility that this subject may cause emotional responses in people and the necessity of working through any emotional responses that rise up within us personally. Also talk about the need to respect and be sensitive to each other over the weeks ahead.

Set week one's homework to read chapters 1 and 2 and think about the questions before the next meeting where you will discuss them.

For each following week

Discuss the questions at the end of each chapter. As a group be aware of what others may be feeling and processing. Remind the group to be respectful and encouraging even if you disagree with another person's opinion – they are allowed to have their opinion. Give them the understanding that any opinion is usually just our current perspective in our growth journey and that we should be open to our opinions changing as more revelation or understanding comes.

At the end of the evening - Set the next week's assignment; to read the next chapter and think through the questions at the end of the chapter. Remember also to pray for the group or any individuals that need to be ministered to before finishing for the night.

Week 2 – Introduction and chapters 1 & 2
Discuss the questions at the end of chapters 1&2 and at the end of the evening pray for each other and set next week's assignment – to read chapter 3, 'Consequences of the Fall' – and think through the questions at the end of the chapter.

Week 3 – Chapter 3 – Consequences of the fall
Discuss the questions at the end of chapter 3 and at the end of the evening pray for each other and set next week's assignment – to read chapter 4 "Before Jesus" – and think through the questions at the end of the chapter.

Week 4 – Chapter 4 – Before Jesus
Discuss the questions at the end of chapter 4 and at the end of the evening pray for each other and set next week's assignment – to read chapter 5, "Jesus, Back to the Original Plan"' – and think through the questions at the end of the chapter.

Week 5 – Chapter 5 – Jesus, back to the original plan
Discuss the questions at the end of chapter 5 and at the end of the evening pray for each other and set next week's assignment – to read chapters 6 and 7 "the Early Church" and "Paul's Tricky Verses" – and think through the questions at the end of the chapter.

Week 6 – Chapter 6 – The early Church and Chapter 7 Paul's tricky verses

Discuss the questions at the end of chapters 6 and 7, and at the end of the evening pray for each other and set next week's assignment – to read chapter 8, "From Jesus and Paul to Today" – and think through the questions at the end of the chapter.

Week 7 – Chapter 8 - From Jesus and Paul to today

Discuss the questions at the end of chapter 8 and at the end of the evening pray for each other and set next week's assignment – to read chapter 9, "Where we are Today" – and think through the questions at the end of the chapter.

Week 8 – Chapter 9 - Where we are today

Discuss the questions at the end of chapter 9 and at the end of the evening pray for each other and set next week's assignment - to read chapter 10, "Into the Future" - and think through the questions at the end of the chapter.

Week 9 – Chapter 10 - Into the future

Discuss the questions at the end of chapter 10 and at the end of the evening pray for each other and share that next week's meeting (the last in this study) you will be having a general discussion about how to proceed with the information you've received in this study, how it can be put into practice in your lives. Let the group know that you will also spend some time praying for each other and releasing each other into the freedom to follow God's call on their lives.

Week 10 – Final week

As a group discuss what you've learnt in this study and the implications and practical outworking of it as individuals and as a group. Share about the possible need for repentance and apology to any people we have slighted, looked down on, spoken badly to etc. as a result of our previous attitudes in regards to this subject, including spouses, family members congregations etc. Spend some time praying for each other, blessing and releasing people into being free to follow God's call on their lives.

Lyn Packer

Lyn Packer has many years of experience as a pastor, prophet, and itinerant minister. She is the facilitator of the New Zealand Prophetic Network and a member of the New Zealand Prophetic Council. Lyn is also the founder and leader of Together Network – a support and resourcing network for women in ministry leadership roles in New Zealand. Lyn also serves on the Global Board of Patricia King's, Women in Ministry Network.

Lyn's ministry is catalytic, setting people free to follow the call of God on their life. As a speaker and teacher her heart for God and her love for people are very evident, as well as her solid understanding of Scripture. Her prophetic and teaching gifts are expressed through a variety of means from speaking to writing and art. She regularly mentors and trains emerging prophets and prophetic ministers through both her online mentoring groups and in national training schools. Lyn is also an author, speaker and artist. As a galleried artist Lyn's work has appeared in group and solo exhibitions and she runs regular prophetic art workshops. She has written books covering a variety of subject matter – prophecy and revelation, creativity, dance, prayer and two books of prophetic allegories. All these books are available on Lyn and Rob's website as listed below:

Websites and contact information
www.robandlyn.org *email* - lyn@robandlyn.org
www.nzpropheticnetwork.com *e-mail* - office@nzpropheticnetwork.com
www.togethernetwork.co.nz *email* - office@togethernetwork.co.nz

www.ingramcontent.com/pod-product-compliance
Lightning Source LLC
LaVergne TN
LVHW011722060526
838200LV00051B/2996